ONCE UPON A TRAIN

4 DECADES OF A WORKING LIFE ON THE VICTORIAN RAILWAYS

DENNIS DENMAN

First published by Ultimate World Publishing 2023
Copyright © 2023 Dennis Denman

ISBN

Paperback: 978-1-922982-60-5
Ebook: 978-1-922982-61-2

Dennis Denman has asserted his rights under the Copyright, Designs and Patents Act 1988 to be identified as the author of this work. The information in this book is based on the author's experiences and opinions. The publisher specifically disclaims responsibility for any adverse consequences which may result from use of the information contained herein. Permission to use information has been sought by the author. Any breaches will be rectified in further editions of the book.

All rights reserved. No part of this publication may be reproduced, stored in or introduced into a retrieval system, or transmitted in any form, or by any means (electronic, mechanical, photocopying, recording or otherwise) without the prior written permission of the author. Any person who does any unauthorised act in relation to this publication may be liable to criminal prosecution and civil claims for damages. Enquiries should be made through the publisher.

Cover design: Ultimate World Publishing
Layout and typesetting: Ultimate World Publishing
Editor: Marinda Wilkinson

Ultimate World Publishing
Diamond Creek,
Victoria Australia 3089
www.writeabook.com.au

Disclaimer. All recollections and opinions are solely those of the author. Comments and timelines during many experiences are supported by FOI documents and personal history records. Many thanks to Nick Anchen for permission to include sections from *Life on the Victorian Railways*.

To another generation, Judd, Mika and Xara. Hopefully their work life will include an adventure or two.

This book is dedicated to the many men in blue overalls who shared their skills, knowledge and stories. Among these characters were some whose names are long forgotten that helped shape a boy's interest in social change and learning ... my appreciation and thanks. On reflection, wins and losses are part of all careers. Each enabled an astonishing variety of roles and challenges across my working life, from my days as an apprentice to the last hurrah.

BEFORE THIS JOURNEY – 1952

It was approaching dusk as I peered between the crowds of people gathered at Ballarat station. Eight-year olds, regardless of their gene pool, are mostly small, and although tall for my age, at eight that was me … a little kid.

On the platform, I could see parts of the large engine, royal blue with a yellow face and stripes along the side. It was at the front of a long, long train.

Suddenly I was whisked away from my parents and lifted into the driver's cabin and dumped on the seat. 'You can see it all from here son,' said a friendly voice. Kneeling on the seat I could see the closed rail gates ahead and outside the cab's side window my parents' smiling faces. 'Let's give 'em a surprise youngster', said the voice as I was steadied on the seat. 'Pull that down,' said the voice, pointing at a wide string called a lanyard. So I did. A joyous cry rang around the platform as the electric horn cried its greeting. 'Again.' So, I did.

Although that experience was not the reason I submitted an application to join the Victorian Railways less than 10 years later, it remains vivid in my memory. Like much else in life, their acceptance was nothing more than chance, but it was the beginning of a journey on the rails that would span four decades and create a lifetime of memories.

CONTENTS

Before This Journey – 1952 — v
Chapter 1: Where it Began – January 1961 — 1
Chapter 2: Jolimont Workshops – The Red Brick Building — 7
Chapter 3: The Train Lighting Depot – The Large Tin Shed — 29
Chapter 4: Newport Workshops – The City Within a City — 43
Chapter 5: The Electrical Engineering Branch – Flinders Street — 61
Chapter 6: Return to Newport – Doors Are Opening — 73
Chapter 7: Overalls to Dust Coat – A Roving Commission — 89
Chapter 8: Sub-Foreman – View From the Other Side — 99
Chapter 9: Electrical Training Centre – A New Calling — 105
Chapter 10: Corporate Training and MURLA – Suits and Ties — 123
Chapter 11: Beyond MURL – Customer Relations — 135
Chapter 12: Princes Gate Staff Training Centre – The Bunker — 147
Chapter 13: State Transport Authority – 67 Spencer Street — 155
Chapter 14: Transport House – Priority Projects — 165
Chapter 15: Rescued - V/Line Projects, Met Trains & Metcard — 187
Chapter 16: Hillside Trains – Last Hurrah — 225
Postscript — 238

CHAPTER 1

WHERE IT BEGAN – JANUARY 1961

From the minute I entered the corridor on the second floor of the Flinders Street rail building, the ripple of noise led the way. My destination was a large room, a ballroom in fact, overlooking Elizabeth Street. On this day, there was not a gown in sight – the room was spilling over with young men about my age.

The noise of shuffled feet and voices surged and waned as questions and queries bounced around the auditorium like drones returning to the hive. Individuals moved between and among the setting of the hundreds of chairs arranged to seat this influx of eager young men. Looking left and right I was a little concerned by the absence of a friendly face. The only solution was to find a vacant chair and let this activity swirl around me as I waited.

ONCE UPON A TRAIN

I sat clutching the security of my paperwork as I took a large breath. Another chapter commenced. Well maybe that's a bit dramatic, but the security of classmates at Swinburne Junior Technical School was now behind me. New personalities lay ahead. Among this throng of possibly two hundred young men I sat, a little intimidated, facing the welcoming committee on stage.

In today's terms this welcoming committee were senior representatives of the Victorian Railways (VR) charged with the immediate induction of these new additions to the workforce. Some faces were recognised as part of the selection panel along with the soon to be introduced Supervisor of Apprentices, the Principal of the Victorian Railway College and a Commissioner.

As I penned these words it all sounded right to me, but memory is a fickle creature and, in this case, elusive. Take two. Yesterday I found myself at the Prahran Mechanics Institute Victorian History Library Inc. and I discovered the day's events had been faithfully recorded in the *VR Newsletter* of January 1961, on page 18.

> 'Welcome – VR Commissioner E P Rogan with Members of the Apprentices Board of Selectors, Messer's W Walker (Member of Staff Board and Chairman of Selection), K A Smith Engineer, Ways & Works, A Chalmers Rolling Stock staff selection and W E Elliot General Secretary, VRI (Victorian Railway Institute).
>
> *For 219 lads, January 16, was a significant day, chosen from 579 applicants, they were apprentices starting their VR careers. It was a record intake of apprentices in the department's history. Warmly greeting the lads at the VRI ballroom, Commissioner Rogan congratulated them on choosing a tradesman's career because with the present technical progress their employment scope was*

WHERE IT BEGAN – JANUARY 1961

greater than ever. Mr Roy Curtis, Supervisor of Apprentices and the Secretary of the VRI completed the welcome.

So here I was. I had followed the directions sent to candidate electrical apprentice Dennis Joseph Denman to report on the 16th of January 1961. Naturally this date is significant to my memory but four days later on the 20th, John F Kennedy was inaugurated as the 35th president of America. I was allocated to the Rolling Stock Branch and didn't at the time link electrical work with trains. A sure indicator of how green I was. Naturally, it didn't enter my head as I was now employed. The young men who shared this day, I would later hear came from towns and regions across the state. We were a huge cross-section of young men and some boys, most at 14 years of age with the minimum of the junior certificate. Nearly all would have been a product of the state's technical college system that ran parallel to the high school system. Each were now bound to a trade

Flinders Street Station from Elizabeth Street (2020)

apprenticeship that was to last five years and cover a wide range of occupations: welders, boilermakers, fitter and turners, electrical fitters (signals and communication), motor mechanics and more. Other occupations were rail oriented such as carriage builders, painters, sail makers, tarp and rope makers and upholsterers to name a few. Along with other instrumentalities, the state was a major force in trade training. At 16, having completed an intermediate certificate in Form 4, I was possibly among the oldest group of this intake and eager for the independence that came with income.

This is my story of one individual among an army of employees that serviced and operated the state's rail services. At the time, I would never have guessed that the VR employees numbered over 33,000 and listed among its activities was the Mt Buffalo chalet, oil lines, hostels and real estate with land and houses at hundreds of statewide locations. My knowledge at this time was limited to aspects of the suburban system and the Flinders Street Station entrance diagonally across from St Paul's Cathedral. The expression 'to meet on the steps at Flinders Street' was to generations of Melbournians as familiar as the Trevi Fountain was to the locals of Rome.

Not to forget 67 Spencer Street, where the Victorian Railways Head Office stood with all its majesty. To the passer-by it may have resembled a stack of structurally arranged granite blocks, several storeys high and set to the footpath edge. Imposing, as early nineteen century architecture could be, it was dull without personality and lost far from the city centre. While we all attended our medical exam there, unfortunately, no recollection of that medical can be recalled, but the CMO (Chief Medical Officer) was the final part of the selection process. In the case of electrical and operating staff it was important that we were not colour blind. The Ishihara colour test was mandatory for certain work grades, as they must be able to decipher the difference between red and green. Obviously, all operations staff and electrical trades are clear examples. One for the aspects of light signals, the other for colour-coded circuitry.

Grand Central Apartments formally Victorian Railways head office (2022)

History notes the story of rail transportation in the State of Victoria was dotted with highs and lows, as communities cried out for connection. Past populations, energised by statewide gold rushes, opened up town after town across the state. Transport of many forms followed, but rail was the giant of the early part of the century.

Combining their needs for services and supply, still others required access to markets and the major ports. The yearly grain harvest was among the highest priority, where spur lines crisscrossed the state and numbered in their hundreds. Posters of the day advertised the cause.

> *Transport – the Vital Link, between the producer and his market, the merchant and his customers. The railway is the best way.*

The Victorian Railways had been a successful instrumentality of government as developing regions demanded access to transport for goods and services. From inception, transport was always a major portfolio and my apprenticeship commenced with Arthur Warner as the Minister for Transport for the second Bolte government. Rail historians note that the early rail freight and parcel services had been a monopoly, but like the demise of steam, the competition of road and air services changed the practices of the past. In Melbourne, the suburban system had slowly radiated from the central city and by 1923 was mostly electrified. This conversion soon realised increased patronage that was to peak and then decline in later years. From the mid-1950s the face of the suburban rail commuter services changed as the steel body blue Harris trains gradually replaced the wooden body Tait trains. Commuters on the Ringwood/Lilydale and Glen Waverley lines were among the first to experience these updates to suburban rail travel. Line by line the red rattlers were condemned for scrap.

Yet the origins of rail and its expansion is of little interest to young men commencing their initial steps in a work situation. Full of enthusiasm they might be, but their interest lay in starting a career, the wheels of the day, the shape of young women's breasts and the operation of a bra J-hook.

CHAPTER 2

JOLIMONT WORKSHOPS – THE RED BRICK BUILDING

After our welcome and the minutia of employment was signed away, I was told to report to the chief clerk at Jolimont workshops. These workshops were not altogether unknown to me. In earlier years together with my friends we had walked the length of Batman Avenue to listen at soapbox or poets' corner to speakers on the Yarra's north riverbank. The red bricks and size of this building dominated the skyline as trams originating from Wattle Park cruised by. Naturally long before social media, but these were different times and entertainment was where you found it.

Surprisingly trains were not my normal mode of transport, for the spur to Kew had been closed in the mid-fifties. The Kew station and line had been linked to the Hawthorn station and fell to heightened property prices and increased road usage. Its last regular passenger service had ceased in August 1952 so I was never to experience a 'local'. Like most communities, the car had long condemned aspects of public transport to city workers, school students and those challenged by economics. Without a car in the family, I was comfortable with the other mode of public transport, the tram. The suburb of Kew was fortunate in having both a bus and tram service linked to Melbourne city. In 1961 the tram service through Kew was part of the North Balwyn line and Mont Albert line passing through Kew Junction. Each line followed different paths to the city with the No. 48 via Bridge Road, Richmond aligned to Flinders Street passing the station before terminating the length of Spencer Street at Latrobe Street.

The No. 42 or 40 from Mont Albert travelled through the length of Victoria Street via North Richmond to Collins Street. Either service aboard the W7 class green and yellow trams made the 10-minute foot race down Batman Avenue to the workshops an easy on-time appointment. From the Swanston Street/Batman Avenue corner it was all downhill to the workshops. I would have passed a corner kiosk, and then, hidden behind a high fence line, the suburban drivers' and guard's depot. Further along the site of the VR garage, the Frank Beaurepaire Pool, much later to be renamed the State Swimming Centre and the Children's Law Courts.

Jolimont was an adjacent suburb to Melbourne city, with the rail yard and workshops consuming a huge wedge of land bordered east by Brunton Avenue and Flinders Street, with Batman Avenue following the line of the river towards Richmond. The Jolimont workshops were located at the eastern end of this huge land track. The workshops dominated the site, an assembly of three buildings with the main building and offices on the southern or river side.

JOLIMONT WORKSHOPS – THE RED BRICK BUILDING

Designated as the lifting shop it was cavernous and high-roofed, some 183m x 18m and the main repair centre for the suburban rail fleet. Immediately to the north and adjacent was the inspection shop where daily light maintenance and inspection took place. This area was serviced by nine tracks, all with inspection pits and recorded as 122m x 37m in size. Behind that and slightly to the Richmond end was the painting and varnishing bays with five tracks, all equipped with overhead platforms. Behind those was the carriage wash dock, completing the diversity of functions for the suburban fleet.

My arrival at the workshops is fairly clouded but all new starts and visitors must report to the office. The signage is clear and our minder passed us along the line. I had arrived with two other apprentices who informed me they were apprenticed electrical fitters. John and David were to be my immediate peers at the start and during my time at Jolimont.

The beginning of my career shared parallels with the commencement of many a working life. In my case it was a journey into the unknown. It was a world of men with all their good-natured banter and competition for work status, where youth are lorded over by men as they move into a generational pecking order established by organisational type. Add another language unique to many industries and professions, sprinkle in every variety of profanity, and this other world takes shape and your actual induction begins.

If you come from a large family, you understand where you fit in, even when your journey has just begun. The mini hierarchy in the VR placed an apprentice within the trade level for the future, above the trade's assistant and labourer, and at tail's end, a lad trainee. Consider five levels (years) of apprentices and John, David and I had to quickly find our feet and a level of comfort. To new eyes, a bustling enterprise, but in the weeks ahead another world was to unfold. The railway industry was facing high levels of competition with limited funding, while introducing the latest technologies and practices. It was the early sixties, 1961 to be precise, and the Vietnam War had been part of the news cycle without Australia's involvement. My generation had embraced and grown up with rock & roll blaring from our transistors and it continued the beat of our generation. Elvis Presley was the king but Col Joy, Johnny O'Keefe and others carried the Australian Flag.

'Well, son this is what you do'

We had been allocated a departmental number that was our identifier for all correspondence and any other issues: my number was 15026. Following the issue of overalls, we were taken on a brief tour of the immediate amenities. Each was allocated a locker in the change room adjacent to the large meal room. Next, we were shown the toilet block and canteen area and a humungous time clock. This time clock, the clerk pointed out, was the in/out point and register of your work time. So, another number was to be added to my new-found collection. This enabled the timekeepers to log your hours of attendance to your pay rate. Payday was confirmed as fortnightly and we would receive a pay slip from our supervisor the day before. For youths who had previously answered a roll call with the occasional flippant comment, this was an entry to a new world.

Time clock held at VR Museum, Williamstown (2022)

The time clocks were set at waist height with a face about 3 feet (1 metre) in diameter with numbers at about an inch (2 cm) apart. To clock on required moving an external swing arm to the position of your clock number and then pushing down.

This action scored a card and effectively signed you in to work. This process occurred again at shift end. Long before the development of proximity cards this 19th century technology was still used by the industry. Accepted as normal, it was possibly a small indicator of a class system between the workforce and the clerical workforce that signed in and out in a book. Alternatively, it was an inherent system that worked with mass numbers. At shift end the workforce lined up to use the time clocks (two in number) much like a sheep run, the image of the jostling and rush to depart the premises at day's end remains a distant but clear memory. Think of the MCG with only one turntable or entrance point with hundreds of men seeking entry with a minute before the ball is bounced and the picture will become clear.

Why Jolimont workshops was my selected location was unclear, but like those previously mentioned sheep I fell in line. Shortly after the induction this newly formed threesome were separated to commence at different locations. I was led among the carriages to what I was to later learn was the wall section. John disappeared towards the stairs and David towards what he would later confirm as the test area. The first impressions are one of size, rapidly followed by the noise. Industry, I was to learn, combined engine noise, rattles, equipment movement, warning signals of whistles and shouts along with the flash of welding strikes. The workshop's main area was the lifting shop with rail tracks linking access from both Richmond and the city end. Over four of these bays and working pits were two overhead gantry cranes.

On the river side of the workshops was a mezzanine level and below that various sections including electric motor repair, the supervisor's office and welding bays. This was to be my home for the next 12 months and my introduction to this industry and the characters of the workforce.

So, what did I bring as part of my skill set? I understood basically that income was the reward for work. I was 16 years old, fit and tall for my age and had undertaken electrical practice and wiring among my final year subjects. A technical school is broadly the extension of primary school but introduces varying trade

JOLIMONT WORKSHOPS – THE RED BRICK BUILDING

Jolimont workshops, lifting shop

experiences and skills in the making of and products of materials – wood, steel, non-ferrous metals, plastics, etc. I had undertaken a morning paper round for years previous, rain, hail, in all weathers, yet nothing prepared me for this and the following days.

The wall section

At the 'wall' I was introduced to a fat man in an open grey dustcoat, Don, and he related that I would be working with Eric and would meet the others between breaks or when working with them. Eric was short and stocky with curly black hair. He was currently working on a M (motor) car and we would be replacing resistance grids and cabling.

As I joined him, my immediate surrounds were as follows. Along the wall were personal lockers and a few hand washing stations but generally fairly bare of character. This area's past records reveal it was part of the four repair tracks and three inspection pits serviced by compressor airline and pit lighting. The two overhead cranes were 25 ton (imperial weight) that ran the full length of the shops. The fitting bays were 137m x 18m, and separated by a carriage length, were a number of suburban rail cars sitting on pedestals approximately a metre or so above floor or ground level. These were located above long pits that enabled the workforce access to all undergear equipment and electrical components. Basically, the system of repair worked along a process line. A defective motor carriage (M car) would be shunted from a train and then into the Shops. This carriage would be separated from its bogies and then lifted into position in the lifting shop. The motors would be removed from the bogies and after steam cleaning forwarded to the motor section for a total refit. On the mezzanine floor motor components such as resistor grids, coils and armatures would be repaired and returned to the motor section for the rebuild.

Red trains, blue trains

A suburban train is basically a five-carriage unit with a M (motor car) at each end and in the centre, and two trailer cars. Note the Harris trains originally ran as seven-carriage sets (M-T-T-M-BT-T-M) reducing to four-car sets off-peak. Other carriage unit sets would occur in the future. Essentially none of this was part of our induction. I had been informed of the basic environment and knew which tradesman I would be working with. The terms of electrical equipment now needed to be mixed with rail talk or operations terminology. An 'up and down' train had meaning, so to 'stabling locations' and 'platform designations'.

JOLIMONT WORKSHOPS – THE RED BRICK BUILDING

In later years, I read of a group of blind men who were each led to a different part of an elephant. The individual feeling the trunk had a vastly different impression of this entity as the one touching the elephant's ear, the one on the side, the other on his tail and so forth. Of course, this example is limited as we (new employees) all had our full senses but it sort of confirms the narrowness of our induction to our immediate role in a part of a very large organisation.

Half an hour later, I was in work mode and assisting Eric Benaim to unfasten cabling and various clamp and connection points. The M car's major electrical components are the compressor, the dynamotor and various grid and resistance banks utilised as part of the motor speed control. Inside the carriage is the driver's cab and equipment fronting the passenger section with the light banks, incandescent in the remaining Tait units and fluorescent tubes in the Harris. Faults or light failure may require a ballast exchange or tube replacement. Top side, on the roof the high voltage power is received via the pantograph to the car. This was to become the daily staple work lot as the Jolimont workforce went about servicing the rail fleet. A certain amount of variety was mingled with carriage types that had updates and slightly different equipment fitting. Dirt and grime combined with manual handling and grunt were a normal part of the trade and a worm's eye of the world from the pit.

Another view of these times is shared by John Bradley, who joined the Victorian Railways in February 1964. John started his working life as a lad trainee at Jolimont workshops and related his early experiences in a section of Nick Anchen's book *Life on the Victorian Railways*:

> '*I began working in the lifting shop at Jolimont with the electricians. I worked in the pit underneath the carriages, armed with a wire brush and my job was to brush the brake dust away from the jumper cables and so on.*'

> *'Everything was fully caked with dust from the cast iron brake blocks and it was a filthy, dirty job, stuck down there in the pit, and I hated it.'*

Manual handling and working safely with lifting equipment became a necessary skill to be learned. In 1961 certification of the workforce to sling equipment had not been introduced and each apprentice, including myself learnt by rote, in other words, this sling or eye bolt will carry this weight for lifting or movement.

Garbed in all manners of either boiler suits or bib and brace overalls, some preferring jeans and old shirts, the meaning of the blue-collar worker became apparent. The sight of highly polished shoes was recognition that the manager or engineer was approaching or at hand, the conclusion of some sort of bush telegraph system operating the moment they hit the workshop floor. The manager's name is lost in the fog of time, but Charles Hansford was the assistant workshop manager. Along social chit chat Eric confirmed he was also a resident of Kew and I could hitch a ride home anytime with the occasional pick up. Within this section I soon become conversant with the others, mostly tradesman and other apprentices in their third and fourth year. They were to provide much insight into life beyond Jolimont, but that was months away.

They were a rich group of personalities and very political as the rail unions did not see eye-to-eye with Premier Bolte and the presiding government. Among the long-remembered personalities who knew the trade backwards was the little digger, Jack Owens. He was that in size and spirit and provided a nice counterpoint to most of his peers. Brown as a berry with his rollings either stuck to his lip or exhaling smoke, he epitomised the Australian character from yesteryear. He, along with some others, was a returned serviceman and had fought behind the lines in Borneo and New Guinea and would hate the 'japs' to his dying day. In his early forties, he brought to light the real language of the past which today is sadly missed. Terms like, 'cobber' and 'mate' were staples with meaning, having a 'fag' was normal, 'ridgy-didge' and 'gidday' lighted every greeting. They were easy men to work with and not one wore the concern that younger men would take over their jobs. At the time the mainstay of conversation among the workforce was whether to accept the government proposal of a service gratuity which amounted to about 1 pound and 30 shillings ($3). The decision would come at some cost as they were to reduce their superannuation contribution and units held to a maximum of 4 units. It was a distracting period with the benefits of money in hand against a degree of security from the pension in retirement. The unions were caught in the cleft of advice and individuals lost in the weight of information. As apprentices we were out of the loop as the proposal did not impact our terms of employment.

Not for you son

My first run in with authority (my boss) was approaching day one shift end. I had been told that a first whistle would indicate five minutes to shift's end and we could wash up and change. Without regard for the first whistle, I had approached the hand trough as the boss cleaned up. 'Not for you son, wait for the first whistle'. Perplexed, I did as I was asked to later learn that the majority of the workforce disappeared much earlier and had buckets and towels stashed in carriages and in hideaways. A minor event but a small indicator of the environment a new employee was introduced into. The second whistle indicated the workforce could queue and clock off. The workshop whistle, rumored to be a WW2 air raid siren, that signaled the start and end of the day shift was reputedly heard by the residents of the surrounding suburbs and the inner city.

Sink or swim is an expression of fact

Quickly the routine of day-to-day unit exchange and testing became the norm and added to this I was enrolled to commence my apprenticeship schooling at RMIT (Royal Melbourne Institute of Technology). RMIT had been established as the Working Men's College in 1887 and was granted the prefix Royal in 1954. The then campus was located in the block bound between Swanston and Latrobe streets, on the western side, the main entry point and administration was at Bowen Street. This was years before it merged with the College of Decoration and Design and amalgamated with the Emily McPherson College of Domestic Economy. In 1994 it was granted the status of a university, becoming the Royal Melbourne Institute of Technology University. Training commenced one day a week and subjects ranged from electrical theory to practice. These building block units were the forerunners to advanced levels over the following years. In 1961 my first year subjects were recorded as:

> Electricity & Magnetism old, Electric Wiring Practice old, Electrical Fitting 1 Theory, Electrical Fitting 1 Practice, Electric Wiring 1 Theory old, Electric Wiring 1 Practice old, Trade Drawing 11, Electrical Fitting 11 Theory and Electrical Fitting 11 Practice.

JOLIMONT WORKSHOPS – THE RED BRICK BUILDING

Author, wiring circuitry board (RMIT, 1961)

Additionally, I had elected to undertake a unit in basic electronics one night a week leading (hopefully) to a technician's qualification. Regrettably this level was not achieved but an enthusiastic start. Yet some things, such as the electrical resistor colour code rhyme remain forever to taunt my memory.

'Bright boys rave over young girls but veto getting wed.'

This translates to Black, Brown, Red, Orange, Yellow, Green, Blue, Violet, Grey and White with resistance values 0–9.

It also marked a long day, as work commenced at 07:26 and classes, on the one day of night school ended at 19:30 to arrive home an hour later.

During the first three months, John, David and I had bonded, taking meals together and we continually found time to explore the workings of Jolimont. John was working on repairing armatures and coil winding. As a frequent visitor I was able to observe the processes of motor repair and the seeming different interpretation of an electrical fitter to electrical mechanic. On one particular day I arrived to listen to an old fitter explaining the difference between mild and chromium steel. He lifted a shaft key and ran it under his nose, remarking, 'It's mild steel, I can tell by its smell.' John and I exchanged looks and took a sniff as requested. We both shook our heads as he said, 'you'll learn' and strode off, leaving two confused apprentices. My comment of 'bullshit' was later supported as a favorite ruse for new kids on the block. Where John was involved in actual equipment repair, I was basically involved in unit exchange.

Upstairs, downstairs

This section located on the mezzanine floor was accessed by stairs at each end of the gallery. This level could also be accessed by a service lift for heavy equipment movement and to access the upper store. It was from the gallery where both John and I learnt one of many small lessons. David was working in the test centre where all forms of high voltage testing was undertaken before motors and equipment were certified as electrically safe. Literally directly below was a section of the gallery where we could shout between ourselves. On this day we were dropping large light globes to which David would catch and stack. Smart alecs that we were, we decided to drop a number at a time for reaction. The globes, which were 300 watt and about 10 inches (25cm +) in length, overpowered those below as we had anticipated. Hitting the concrete floor out of reach they literally exploded with a deafening bang. Unfortunately,

JOLIMONT WORKSHOPS – THE RED BRICK BUILDING

the effects of this simple prank caused a minor riot below as the test electrician had experienced bomb trauma during the blitz in London. He was not impressed with the explosions near his workstation. We copped the abuse and quickly apologised and sought to find less injurious distractions.

Freedom to roam was as simple as carrying an electrical component in hand or a requisition for parts from the storehouse. In most cases it was for a chat but occasionally it was because the tradesman needed to disappear. 'Keep out of sight' or 'finish up these connections, I'll be back in a couple of hours.' Added to these times aplenty, we observed the other aspects of business. The pathway to 'Snowy' the bookmaker who took bets from a shilling (10 cents) to a pound ($2) never interfered with work. Snowy also was a short-term money lender to the few workers who were always short from pay to pay. As the industry was paid fortnightly the lesson of money management was promptly learned but some were looking for loans within days. The loan rate was unknown. His offsider, we were told, could supply any type of condom for a price.

Haircuts were available at different spots for 2 shillings (20 cents) during lunch and the new meaning of a 'foreigner' became clear. Everything and anything could be either repaired or replaced by the skill and resource base of the workshops. For those with long established connections to the 'honeypot' at Newport workshops, anything could be done. Larger facilities meant more diverse skills in pattern making, a foundry and machining, depending on the need or who you knew. Although much was done in meal break periods even the noise of the whistle was not a deterrent to busy timelines. Car servicing and odd jobs were part of the lunchtime break. Stories of an individual signing on and working as a barman in Flinders Street before returning to sign off were conjecture but alas among the tales. And tales there were – of a lad trainee caught masturbating in the privacy of a carriage, the rush to initiate a new lad by rubbing grease and sawdust into his privates were an ever-present threat, the gallons of paint missing from inventory, and the sinker moulds that continually consumed white metal and lead from carriage floorplates. This was the other side of industry.

Downstairs

Within three months David and I changed places and the test bed became my next workstation. Working for another small man in stature and forgotten by name, he was industrious and busy and safety was his catchphrase. Explaining the danger of HV (high voltage) testing and working in this environment required smarts and clear process. Advice well received and between testing and small equipment repair, work time passed quickly. During this period, we watched on as an incident was minimised due to smarts and fortune. A painter working on the face of a wall over balanced and hung precariously as a local supervisor had the foresight to move one of the travel cranes into position. From the crane platform a rescue occurred. The smarts were attributed to one Billy Cox whom I was to meet many years distant as a key player in safety.

Beyond the workshop's fence the other memorable event of this period was the down tools and boycott of a Japanese Industry study group that were supposedly to tour the workshops. Although they had previously met with senior Victorian Railway officials (the May 1961 edition of the *VR Newsletter* references the Japanese study group) they never entered the shops. Nearly 20 years on from the Japanese bombing of Pearl Harbour and Darwin, many of the workshop population would never forget or forgive. Years later as an adult I was to read about Sir Ernest Dunlop and POWs on the Burma Railway and Changi. My thoughts these many

JOLIMONT WORKSHOPS – THE RED BRICK BUILDING

years later were of the many untold stories and the generations who never healed.

After six months I was relocated to The inspection shop with wider scope and even more freedom within the workday. This was also about tax time and I was confronted with an employee statement of earnings. For the 6-month period, my earning totalled 119 pounds 2 shillings and 10 pence, roughly equivalent to $240. The instructions were clear, please complete the Commonwealth of Australia, Form S, Salary & Wages Return for the period 1st July 1960–30th June 1961. My deductions were minimal, about 3 pounds for tools of trade, screwdriver sets, pliers and side cutters. Once more another number was attached to my name, a tax file number.

The Inspection Shop was geared around inspection and minor repairs that would usually be done in a shift or between peaks. The work sequence typically unraveled as follows: as trains finished the morning peak those designated for inspection via the shop would be brought by the driver to the allocated road. All tracks are raised on concrete bases leaving a space beneath the carriages to make easy access for inspections of the undergear equipment and motors. The pits were about 1.5m wide and deep enough for the average male to stand in. From there either the driver or electrical fitter would drive them into the shed and locate them to position. Other train sets not due for inspection would gradually fill the Jolimont yard sidings waiting for the evening peak.

I quickly learned why morning arrivals were so anticipated: it was a race to find the booty left behind. Competition between the drivers and various trades were good-hearted and shared. The morning papers first – *The Argus, The Age, The Herald* or *The Sun* – followed by the travelling public's memory losses, umbrellas, bags of all sorts, books, sunglasses, any number of items that should have been located by station staff and sent on to lost property. The larger items would be passed on.

I do have a strong memory of the arrival from Newport workshops of a sparkling new royal blue painted Harris train. I recall the admiration of the welcoming group as this unit arrived outside the shops whether to enter the evening peak or be part of in-service testing is unclear. Records indicate that during the period 1961–1967, 30 of the Harris second series were delivered and built by Martin and King. Possibly, this was a part of the Harris train handover program, but it was my first eyes on. A string of brilliant navy blue catching the sunshine. So memorable.

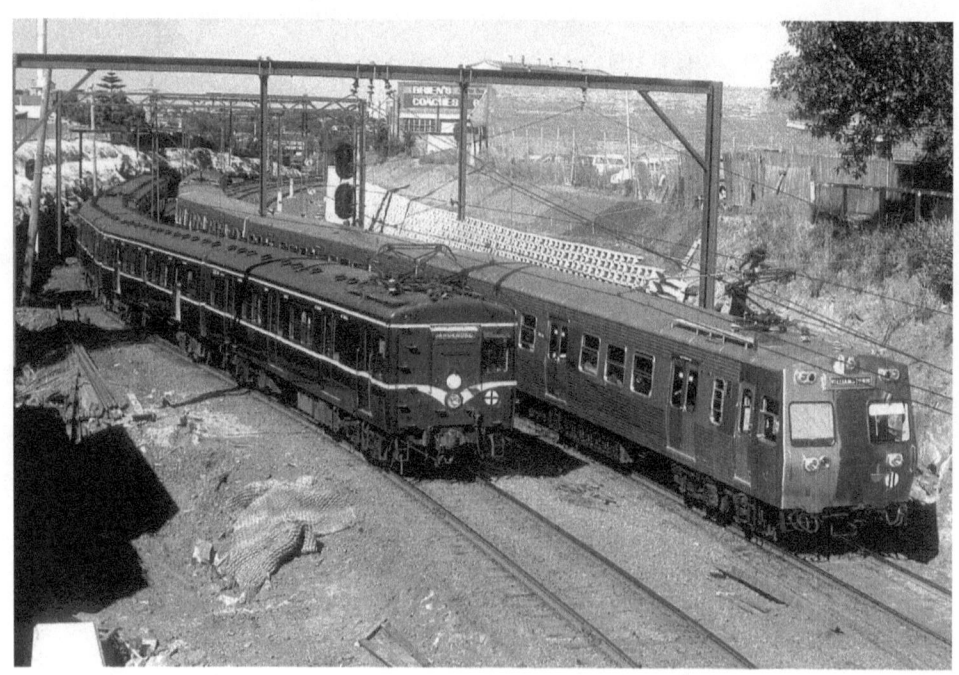

Harris and Hitachi units

JOLIMONT WORKSHOPS – THE RED BRICK BUILDING

Operationally, the red card denoted a major problem and would usually mean a car replacement, due to a hot axle box or motor failure. But more important to the electricians and carriage builders were the driver and guard reports into the smaller complaints, failures and items not working: cab heaters, destination lights, internal light banks, door sticking, window smashed, etc. Any item designated as electrical was the responsibility of the inspection electrical mechanic or fitter and his apprentice … me. The minutiae of train maintenance became varied and time consuming from pantograph pan replacement to traction motor commutator cleaning and brush wear checked or replaced. Perfect work for an apprentice, as squatting in a pit to hold an emery stick over a turning commutator becomes wearisome after the first twenty or so. Seating new brushes also requires a patient hand ignoring the dust and carbon residue. Each maintenance road had a designated power switch that could be locked in the on/off position. Off for non-power applications. The switch had positions for multiple locks. Each trade group would apply their own lock when working. Given some applications, the switch would have a number of locks in place as different trades or applications occurred.

The sign, 'Electricity Kills' was immediately above Danger High Voltage. This signage was not the case in the many stabling yards, as they were open to all weathers and unroofed. Besides electrical inspection and repair, an army of cleaners constantly moved between sets, along with fitters and car builders replacing the odd broken window or seat repair. The time between arrival and the PM peak was around four hours and consumed the major effort. It was also a fitness regime, as going from ground to cab repeatedly tested the leg muscles, a sort of leapfrog system from unit to unit.

For someone exploring a busy social life the occasional rest period in the furthest siding was appreciated … the stabling area for off peak trains was the size of multiple city blocks with designated sidings. The furthest sidings (Hurstbridge and Epping lines) were contained by the boundaries of Flinders Street and enclosed on the east side by Brunton Avenue. The remaining east and south-eastern lines were allocated to the central and Jolimont Yard sidings fronting the workshops. The business was built on turnaround efficiency and meeting the train required for the evening peak.

How we do thing here

The culture of Jolimont was gradually shaping every apprentice to its will. As apprentices we continued our learning phase to tightly regulated work practices and territories clearly defined. Demarcation between trades and roles was entrenched down to the material and head type of a screw, and within the shops the trade barriers of work type were closely maintained. In the yards, the teamwork of the various tradesmen to 'get it done asap' was clearly recognised. The key to our work was a driver's key and a standard 'H' key for doors and opening panels. Here, although some roads could be isolated the majority of times, we required power. Other than the driver's report our role included inspection and repair of all external and internal lamps in every train set. Against the odds of an unexpected shunt a simple metal disc or a red flag was placed in front of the leading cab. Together we would enter the cab by the steps and engage the air held in the compressor reservoirs to raise a pantograph. This enabled power to the train and a 240-volt system by means of an inverter. This was an enjoyable period of work and social life. During this time, I mainly worked with Deita, and a clearer picture of rail electrics and train operations was painted.

JOLIMONT WORKSHOPS – THE RED BRICK BUILDING

Yet I acknowledged the gap between my school subjects and application within the activities of my working day. At RMIT I was learning the applications and circuitry of 240 voltage and two-way switching household circuits and general industry. Trains powered by 1500-volt DC (Direct Current) and via various equipment/devices either regulated to 750 DC traction motors or low voltage activities such as lighting and automatic door closure were quietly pigeon-holed away. Albeit a circuit diagram and symbols will be somewhat similar, train maintenance was by year's end not on my radar. My goal was to qualify as an A grade licence holder which meant working in/on general electrical equipment and locations. This was my work today, the here and now, but not my future pathway.

At the end of the year, I was to report to the Manager, Train Lighting Depot. John remained for another period, and I was told David transferred his apprenticeship to a private contractor nearer his home in Frankston. Transfers within any bureaucracy are fairly impersonal and contain the mere specifics. One location to another is fairly quick with at times a minimum of notice by routine memo. No examples remain of these apprentice years but many others remain of transfers and memos in the years following.

Victorian Railways

R.S. (Rolling Stock) reference   Chief Mechanical Engineer's Office,
                                   Melbourne.   Date.

Memorandum: I have pleasure in advising you….
                                   Chief Mechanical Engineer, W Galletly.

CHAPTER 3

THE TRAIN LIGHTING DEPOT – THE LARGE TIN SHED

My transfer led me to quickly understand another phase in my training, as I basically moved from the suburban fleet to regional and interstate train services. In 1962 most services were maintained at the Train Lighting Depot and yards between Spencer Street and North Melbourne. The TLD as it is usually referred to, was the regional (then country and interstate) carriage maintenance location. Formally the Dudley Street Carriage Depot, TLD is located at the west end of the Spencer Street rail yard with the building configured to several roofed roads providing all weather work access and power/air supplies. Together, with this carriage maintenance function, was the servicing and repair of lead acid batteries. Anyone working in this area was instantly recognised, encased in gum boots an acid limiting leather apron and face shield with elbow to finger-tip gloves. A quick visit was enough for an assault on the senses and a location to be avoided.

My year at TLD was varied, with periods at the VR garage, back to Batman Avenue, the Rail Motor Depot, visits to the North Melbourne Steam Loco Depot and the maintenance roads. During my first few months in between changing out starter motors and generators with the occasional rewire of truck tail-lights, the movement of country train services began to fade. The cars of the day created much discussion and interest as both Ford and GMH dominated the local market. Passing through our doors were the latest models as the government system turned over their fleet. Whether sedans or utes, the Ford Falcon XK and Holden's EJ series turned heads. Located close to the city, lunch periods occasionally extended, cemented to the neo-cortex as the streets of Melbourne became second nature. The pathway of lanes and byways between Flinders Street and Latrobe Street were all explored with distractions at many locations.

My day release program had recommenced, and the first year results were satisfactory without being outstanding or bringing any adverse or complimentary comments. Although I am unable to recall the event, all apprentices would have been consulted by the Supervisor of Apprentices to discuss their report and progress. As I attended RMIT and not the Railway College, it is possible (but unlikely) I was outside the system. My second-year subjects were Electric Wiring 11 Theory old and Electric Wiring 11 Practical old.

THE TRAIN LIGHTING DEPOT – THE LARGE TIN SHED

The return trip to TLD added more tram time to my daily journey. Where for the past 15 months I had exited at Flinders Street for my flight down Batman Avenue, now my destination was the western end of the city. I soon found an alternative to my Collins Street terminus. During the peak period, a few No. 40 trams were timetabled via Latrobe Street enabling my journey direct to Spencer Street and a 5-minute walk down Adderley Street, unlike the bulk of the workforce that exited Spencer Street Station and followed the walkways in the rail yard to the depot.

Further west was the North Melbourne Steam Locomotive Depot and workshops. A fleeting memory remains of a brief period attending the loco depot and assisting in the replacement of engine lights and oddments. The depot which had served its place in rail history was cold, dark and dirty with a hundred years of coal burning residue on every surface. Another view of the times taken from Nick Anchen's book, this time of the loco depot, was a segment by Gordon Arblaster of the earlier years, when he had begun work as an engine cleaner at the depot in 1954:

> 'North Melbourne was quite something. It was a filthy place – absolutely putrid. The smoke and the smells were beyond description, and whenever engines moved around the loop outside the shed, the office shook and vibrated and soot and muck fell on everything.'

A sight unseen and without any of the romance that steam enthusiasts attach for the remnants of this bygone era. Built in 1888 and housing up to 160 locomotives as late as 1950, the new wave of technology confirmed its era supplanted.

Within the shed

To accurately describe the TLD is to imagine a large tin shed open at one end with a series of dedicated tracks from the Spencer Street yard ending at the point of Adderley Street along Dudley Street. Looking back towards the station, possibly 10 roads were roofed by corrugated iron with clear sections for natural light. Each of these roads had wooden plank decking with access to airlines and electrical power services. Floor level was door height of a carriage or train when docked, with access to under gear, electrical equipment and jumper cables beneath these walkways. Our immediate neighbour was the 'House of Stoush' or Festival Hall but I was never to grace its walls for a fight. Years later I attended a concert headlined by Peter, Paul & Mary, great entertainers and folk leaders in the civil rights movement in the USA. For those of a later year the image of a large tin covered shed might be difficult to imagine in a modern city, yet this was the industry of the past. The shed was not only aged, but years of pigeon shit graced every rafter and the smells of excrement and grime was part of every road. Long before the use of sullage tanks most train toilets vented to the track. Remember the sign in country carriages? *Please do not use toilets in station precincts.*

Although industrial safety was visible and practised and roads cleaned, the Occupational Health and Safety Act was many years away (1985).

The introduction of the diesel locomotive in 1951 followed the worldwide trend to greater speed and cost efficiency and condemned the age of steam to the annuals of history. Other major decisions of government during this period were to shape the future of both the industry, and by timing and circumstances, one apprentice, by minor degrees. Twelve months prior (1960)

THE TRAIN LIGHTING DEPOT – THE LARGE TIN SHED

saw the introduction to parliament of the plan for the Melbourne Underground Railway Construction bill and the final stages of the broad gauge linking the capitals of Victoria and NSW. This major milestone was due to be opened in June of 1962. Additionally, recorded in the January 1960 issue of the *VR Newsletter* was an item of a study tour to Germany and France. Mr L C Rolls (Engineer on the staff of the Superintendent of Loco Maintenance) researched the options of the diesel hydraulic locomotive V60 (German Rail) similar to VR 25W class. Some major events within the rail industry and wider world were making headlines.

At different ends of the organisation, change was front and centre. The standard gauge between Sydney and Melbourne was completed to high appraise and the *Inter-Capital Daylight* service commenced. The South Dynon Diesel Locomotive Depot was opened as the use of steam dwindled to remote locations, and by mid-1964, the loco depot was closed.

On the national scene, August 1962 is recorded as the initial deployment of the first Australian regular support troops to Vietnam. The federal Menzies government had joined the United States in their endeavours to hold back the communist threat and the so called 'domino theory'. Yet these decisions of government were miles away and without any personal impact. My immediate concern was to wash away the soot and grime of the steam locos and find my way to the rail motor depot, mid yard at Spencer Street.

Regrettably the individual who took me under his care can only be recalled as helpful and friendly. Here I was introduced to the Walker Rail Motor or Diesel Electric Rail Motor (DERM) as they were commonly known. These had been purchased from Walker Brothers, England and delivered in 1948 with additions over the period to 1955. The car bodies were built locally by Martin and Kings and assembled at the Newport workshops. Electrically the lighting system was 24-volt DC via belt-driven axle generators and our days were spent undertaking the routine of service examinations, lamp replacement and repairs. Soon enough the Walkers were left behind as the fleet at TLD became the priority.

Different but the same

After my tour at the rail motors, I returned to the umbrella of the depot. The 24/7 rhythm of maintaining the regional train units/sets with the priority of the profile services had not paused, including the *Inter-Capital Daylight*, *Spirit of Progress* to Albury, the *Overland* train between Melbourne and Adelaide, and the Mildura service the *Vinelander*. Once more I was to observe the flow of business and the different talents. Not that one individual was smarter than the next regardless of their technical nous. It seemed that some roles required qualities beyond their technical skills. The electrical mechanic who serviced and maintained the country fleet was lower in the pecking order than the individual rostered on the Commissioner's train or the State car, in other words, state governor or royal visits. Similarly, the travelling electrician on the interstate trains handling faults or complaints seemed to have other skill sets, maybe people skills. They understood the nuances of the travelling customer with tales aplenty. I had much still to learn.

Story time

One story (among many) is of *Inter-Capital* customers who complained in one compartment of being too hot, and in the adjacent one of being too cold. After discussions with the conductor and the travelling electrician's assurance that the thermostat setting had been changed the complainants' changed suites and were happy ever after. Stories abounded on the produce returning from these lay-over country locations from fresh eggs to ham on the bone and even a small piglet. The Victorian train crew stayed at Junee with the travelling electrician further into NSW at Harden. This was the produce centre and another insight into the business of transport and variations. On reflection, an endeavour akin to an underground or black market operating in conjunction with train operations. At age 18 I was in the latter part of the second year of my apprenticeship. Day release to RMIT had continued without any meaningful connection to my industry and I was a better draftsman than I was an electrical train specialist. It underlines the relevance of theory to practical if you can't see any connection

Once again, the flurry of business was set into motion as both the *Inter-Capital Daylight* and the Adelaide *Overland* AM arrivals were split and placed into roads of the depot. Then, April 16, 1962, saw the direct interstate service between Sydney and Melbourne commence. The *Southern Aurora* cars from memory were shunted to a location at Dynon. Their arrival from Spencer Street initiated all manner of activities as cleaning staff replaced bedding from the sleeping cars, freshly laundered in and soiled out to the VR laundry. I joined the electrical mechanics and others in checking all conductor reports and connected each half train to the depot's fixed power sources. The power vans which supplied electricity to each train were shunted to fueling points as the train was serviced. A normal day would be the rousting out of the slower members of the team before the allocation of work roles. Different exams for car types against date ranges or usage were daily activities before the priority of the main fleet arrived, the *Inter-Capital Daylight*, the *Overland*, etc.

The *Overland* of the day had distinctive steel sleeping cars catering for individuals and couples. Far ahead of the times for recognising our indigenous people the cars reputedly were named after Aboriginal locations, the roomettes included Allambi, Chalaki and Tantini. The layout of the roomette carriage was a central winding corridor with roomette compartments either side. A customer had a single berth compartment, toilet and wash basin within his compartment and communal showers at each end of the car. The twinettes were totally inclusive with twin berths, shower and toilet. Some of the twinette cars were named Weroni, Yankai and Yanni. All these cars were air conditioned and serviced by a conductor.

Usually, we would meet the train at No. 2 platform and ride it back to the yard for an early sight of work required. Compartment lights were a relatively easy fix, so to an urn in the conductor's compartment, unit change-over or an element to be changed in the depot. Cooling and heating were the bane of our lives, even with filters changed frequently. Testing the thermostats to prove air conditioning efficiency was an ongoing role as the weather cycle varied. It was during this period that I began to observe the pressure of business and some coping mechanisms … albeit some of my own.

Beyond the intercity trains the country sets came and went. The type of country carriage possibly AE and BE categories were all powered/lighted by batteries. Similar to the motor car, the battery voltage is generator-backed by a belt-driven system from the wheel axles. A constant occupation as the cycle of lost, and stretched belts were part of every day's inspection, repair or replacement. The smarter at fault-finding you were, the more challenging the work, and here teamwork came together against operational timelines. Always an exception, but this group were diligent in completing these exams and other cyclic work. Say an A exam would detail a full inspection and test operation sequence, plus cleaning all copper contacts, check and replace copper braids and all fuses.

THE TRAIN LIGHTING DEPOT – THE LARGE TIN SHED

Let's call him Norm, who daily signed off the majority of his exam sheets with little more than a cursory check on opening the panel. Complications ruined his day and could be steadied by the contents of strategically hidden large brown bottles

Not all about trains

The overall manager of the depot by memory was Mr J Deacon (Train Lighting Inspector) but a more memorable character had taken me under his wing, or sort of. His name was Neil McMillian and he was one of the electrical supervisors. Gowned in the garb of a supervisor the traditional grey dustcoat belted at the waist, Neil was of middle height, in his early forties with mischievous twinkling eyes. In the many years of the Marlboro cigarette ads and the like, he favoured a pipe packed with some ubiquitous aromatic brew. Combining both a wry sense of humour and electrical nous, I was to learn a lot about this part of the industry and other life lessons he felt were a necessary part of my training.

Working with different tradesmen, Neil oversaw a variety of my experiences and watched as the temptations for my age group progressed. As may be inferred by this time, the number of the fairer sex visible in the maintenance areas of the industry were minimal. Certainly, women were employed in the typing pools at head office, a few at the larger workshop canteens but beyond that invisible. Not so the depot or adjacent to – female refreshment staff were on buffet cars on most country services. It was here on the refreshment car named the Taggerty normally part of the 12 noon Bendigo to Melbourne service that Neil put me to the sword. Beneath a veil of smoke and with clarity of purpose, he personally introduced me to all of the buffet staff with the promise, if they had any needs ... ask for me. I imagine my ears were tending towards crimson and I was assuredly out of my depth. Just another step in the learning process. Fast tracked to the meal break and over cards would be exchanged the stories of both country and interstate travel experiences. Here amid the food of choice the stories unfolded between the travelling electricians and the depot staff. If there was a hierarchy of sorts it was only about take-home pay.

The travelling show had the bonus of shift and travelling allowances which made for a relatively healthy income and appreciably more than the depot supervisor. Add in any late running, the cream was added to the cake. The other pea position was part of the staff for the Commissioner or State car as it went on regular tour and ceremonial visits. The Governor of Victoria at this time was Sir Reginal Dallas Brooks followed by Sir Rohan Delacombe from May 1963. These key positions elevated the staff of driver, guard, conductor and electrician to recognition above the masses. As for the State car it seemed to be always in upgrade mode for every modern convenience. State car No.4 was old-world opulence with a combination of high, white ornate ceiling, richly timbered surfaces and warm leather seating upholstery. Add to the décor, elegant Queen Anne chairs and plush velvet curtains which complimented both status and comfort. Whether true or a mischievous snippet, one story above all provided high-level mirth around the meal table. An apparent complaint from the State car occupants that the toilet rolls had been placed incorrectly. 'Dear boy,' someone mimicked, 'everyone knows, you roll from the top and not from the bottom.'

Beyond the skuttle involving extracts from the daily papers both interstate and local, a normal lunch period was dedicated to cards, either Euchre or Poker at which I was fairly accomplished. Euchre was a favourite at the family table and played regularly.

THE TRAIN LIGHTING DEPOT – THE LARGE TIN SHED

Typically out of context, according to Luke, Jesus said 'man does not live by bread alone' and this was true at the depot. It seemed that every payday the workforce found their way to the nearest hotels for a counter lunch. In reality it was a daily routine for a few, but again the exception. Prior to turning 18 this was never a consideration, but as my social life expanded, I had gradually shared a glass of porphyry pearl and the odd beer. The Liquor Laws of Victoria prohibited anyone under the age of 18 being served, buying from or being on a licensed premises. Now of age, I could join the group for a lunch. A pleasant but slightly rushed first lunch and the consumption of one beer. This was my baptism to wet lunches and for everyone who ate; most just came for a beer, especially in Melbourne's summer … as I was to observe in my remaining time at the shed.

Observation in and around my environment is part of my psyche and a beer or two might have been recognised as the drug of the time in many industries, including the rail industry.

In Victoria, 6 o'clock closing was the law of the land and this local phenome had been in place since 1916. The 6 o'clock swill would take another five years before being abolished in 1966. The following payday I was asked to join two older apprentices and happily went along. Once more a quick lunch and a single beer as I was conditioned to be back on time. Imagine my surprise as Neil Mc followed me out the pub's door with a general reminder over his shoulder for others, not to be late. What followed on our walk back to the depot was a father-son discussion with my full attention and hidden grin; he expounded on the evils of drink and the pleasures of the fairer sex. I might have told him I had figured out the intricacies of the bra clip with a little help from a gorgeous young woman, but my private life remained just that and never a topic for the workplace. Were my ears red once more? Probably.

With summer's arrival, once more my travel papers arrived for my next location. My second-year results from RMIT were again satisfactory with a string of passes and a couple of exemptions granted by the Board of Studies. The third year of my apprenticeship was to commence at Newport workshops, where I was to report to the Chief Clerk and then on to the plant shop. Looking back these many years later, it might be questioned if the method of training, although providing great overall experience, left you with a sufficient knowledge of either infrastructure or fleet type. There is little doubt that as a base building block I had been provided with a wide experience in the prime functions of the Rolling Stock Branch but seemly without the recognition of my goal to qualify as an A grade electrician (electrical mechanic). Consequently, by exceptions I was not to work on a suburban train for another decade and thoughts of returning to TLD was far removed. Beyond the fog of time, I'm unsure if the activities of my apprenticeship were fully mapped out against some necessary skill set or if it was time allocation to specific locations. Notwithstanding that reflection, I was about to embrace a new location. My journey time to Newport would increase by another 30 minutes and now add a train to my daily tram journey. Another turn of the wheel.

Clock tower, administration centre,
Newport Workshops (2022)

CHAPTER 4

NEWPORT WORKSHOPS – THE CITY WITHIN A CITY

Arriving at my destination of Newport was a new experience, not altogether like a first visit to another city, but uniquely different. The 'shops' were bordered by the Williamstown line on one side and the Altona/Geelong line on the other. This wedge formed a large triangle from Newport Station to the base at Champion Road.

For the 3000-odd workforce regulars arriving by train, they had the option of two destination platforms. Timetabled trains arrived at either the tarpaulin shop platform or the main (or garden) platform adjacent to the clock tower. This Italianate styled three-story edifice towered over the workshop site and adjoining buildings and was the centre point of the enterprise. It contained among its floors the engineering and drafting staff, with the administration and manager's office on the ground floor facing the garden. Records remind me that Mr R Roach was the manager on my arrival. After work, two departure trains serviced the workforce departing the garden platform around 16:15 and 16:30. Nothing better than door-to-door service.

My arrival was timed to the garden platform having made the appropriate connection at Flinders Street. I had travelled in a non-smoking compartment on a Tait train and had counted each station between Flinders Street and Newport before pulling into the shops. Paper work in hand I was quickly processed and pointed in the direction of the plant shop. It was some 400 metres past the stores area and the last building towards Champion Road. Finally, I imagined, I had arrived at my goal where the real work of electrical practice would commence. Once more the procedure of induction occurred watched on by a number of men standing with their backs to a pot belly stove. Summer or winter, but especially winter, this was the gathering point. As their day's work was allocated or they disappeared, I made ready for my start. With my token safely tucked inside my pocket and locker allocated, my surroundings could be taken in.

I should briefly pause to explain a token. About the size of a penny coin, but twice its weight, it was numbered and stamped. This token was lifted by an employee from a peg board before the start time and returned to the board at the end of a shift. Each employee had their own token and another number to add to my list ... the Newport workshop's version of the Jolimont time clock. Another variant of the sheep run was soon at hand with my first payday experience in the plant shop. Pay slips were handed out the preceding day allowing time for queries or a rare mistake.

NEWPORT WORKSHOPS – THE CITY WITHIN A CITY

On the Thursday morning (still paid fortnightly) we queued in alphabetical order at the tool room window to receive a small metal tin that contained our wages. Briefly taken over by the pay office, the tool room for a period held the total plant shop wages defended by two clerks and a holstered pistol. Shades of the wild west but many years before direct payment to bank accounts. The Armaguard delivery enabled cash in a can, in notes and coins, as the order of the day.

The plant shop was a large rectangular building with high sawtooth roofed area and the last section of an extended block of different work functions, including the main storehouse. At one end, was an office, with the length of the building divided into halves, each designated for equipment maintenance and preparing the installation of new plant. On my half, the electrical section, on the other the mechanical fitters. The hierarchy in the office was two electrical supervisors, James Riley and Ron Feigan, and two fitter supervisors, George Smith and Len Smith (no relation) reporting to the Plant Manager or Engineer. The rear of the workshop contained the office of the works sub-foreman of the brickies, Joe Keneally, who oversaw the maintenance of all furnace types (fire bricks) and general site concreting. Of the Newport crew, Joe and George Pearce were to become allies in wider pursuits and were the first to bring the VFL into my social life. Both were Collingwood supporters and George a Collingwood member. In the year ahead I was to enjoy many a Saturday afternoon match at Victoria Park with George, compliments of his guest ticket. Heady days with Thompson palming the Sherrin to Price and hitting a leading McKenna on the chest … goal! History would show that other interests would in time take over in my social life and relegate Collingwood and the VFL.

In some ways I was a little surprised in my immediate environment as not one carriage or wheel was in sight. Yet carriages in various stages of repair or paint fronted every feeder rail line to the various shops. The workshops comprised a large complex of buildings each with a designated work function. I was soon to learn that the workshops rang to the business of carriage construction, major refits, wheel machining and a thousand other functions linking the workforce.

To work to work

The shop workforce was a wide group of nationalities with my peer group mostly Australian and the labouring and trades assistants mostly Southern European. This mix was soon to change. The plant shop was to be my home location for the next 700 plus days and through that time I was rotated through different roles suitable for a third and fouth year apprentice. Once more new work types and experiences confronted me as the images of carriages and sets receded. So, the learning process continued year by year.

From those early times when you have limited skills and know-how, you build your knowledge through a combination of repetitive work and the explanation of those about you. Theory classes merge with anyone from a supervisor to a trade's assistant, many who has mastered the work aspects by observation and prior experience. Soon I was paired with Alfred Pugh and in latter days and weeks commenced the rewiring of main switchboards and equipment. Alfie, or Gramps as I called him, was a warm and friendly personality, below medium height with thinning hair and for his size strong as a bull. His devotion to sunbaking was his summer period preoccupation. Alf was one of a group who had been reclassified to trades level from labourer/trades assistant as part of an in-house (VR) system to overcome manpower and skill shortages in previous years. At the time of my arrival the major role beside day-to-day maintenance was the conversion of the various shops to the 50-cycle power distribution. This supply was via new 22,000 Volt substations and a grid system supplied from the State Electricity Commission (SEC). Historically the workshop's power supply was generated by the Newport substation. Newport A was opened in 1918 to supply electricity as part of the electrification of the suburban rail system by the Victorian Railways. It was a dated 25-cycle system with a red-inked closure date. It was a time of major change within the shops.

The *VR Newsletter* carried the following article in July 1964 describing the change:

> *Good progress has been made in the conversion of the Department's power system from 25- to 50-cycle frequency. To date, more than half the obsolete 25-cycle substation plant has been replaced and augmented by modern 50-cycle plant. So far, the savings made by the conversion amount to 88,000 pounds (estimate $200,000) a year.*

Ongoing for some years but now in full swing, I joined Alf in the timber dressing and wood shop. Mains and switchboards first and then replacing the overhead lighting with new gas-discharged halogen lamps. Every light point required a new circuit and multiple units to a switch. Industry circuits of the day were enclosed in steel conduit and most had to be shortened and threaded by hand. Swinging on a pipe threader soon added a little muscle to my frame. The physical aspects of installing mains cabling encased in 3" piping at ceiling or roof height was demanding and required as much grunt as it did smarts. I was soon to learn the benefits of a block and tackle and chain blocks. Both had their roles in aspects of mechanical lifts for heavy items, water pipes and trunking.

From the turnery to timber shop there was plenty of work. In the timber shop every machine prior to conversion had been driven by a discrete belt system below ground and powered by a number of 25-cycle motors. Unlike any previous experience, I seemed to have strayed back in time, as the older machines gave up their drive systems to be replaced with the modern. The teamwork between the fitters, relocating planers, saws, every type of wood machining equipment, and the electrical staff was apparent, albeit with much disparaging comments. A similar program occurred in the turnery as once more the 50-cycle mains preceded the machine shop requirements as individual lathes, planers, drilling machines and milling machines were changed over with minimum production loss. This was heavy industry and an eye opener.

Getting used to heights

Ladders and heights were to become secondary to our period of improved lighting shop by shop. Our next major program was the tarp shop where again the overhead lighting and sewing machine 50-cycle change over began in earnest. Tarpaulins for open wagon covers were still a major part of the industry. Security lighting was another variation to these themes located external to the buildings. Physically fixed to the outside of the buildings most of the circuitry and unit fixing was undertaken at ladder's end. This high position was also the route of the past steam pipe systems that was lagged in asbestos wrapping. A health hazard not entirely understood by the industry or communicated to the 'plant workforce' of the day. Respirators and safety goggles were recommended, but their benefits soon became lost in the difficulty in the working conditions. The exertion of up and down and ladder repositioning was the go. The respirators constricted your breathing and your sight diminished by vapour on the lens. My recollection remains clear, 50 years on of that puff (a little like smoke) from the asbestos wrapping as the top of the ladder was man handled into place.

The mastermind for all this circuitry changeover should probably be sheeted to the Senior Foreman James McKinlay Riley and his subordinate Ron Feigan. Both were to play significant roles in my skill development. Missing from my 'need to know' would be the engineering department who would have surveyed the shop and prepared plans of machine location and positioning and the aspects of workflow. On reflection, I am reminded of the bubble that we all live within at any time and Newport had become mine. The larger organisation and train operations had disappeared or faded as my work life revolved around a small group of individuals and our support roles. My day release training continued at RMIT and was specific in subjects supporting my future. Additionally, although a dud with electronics I had enrolled in a supervisor's course at RMIT and found the units stimulating. Unknown as to the why at the time, and never a thought of a clean hands' future. An A grade licence was years away. An applicant must be 21 years of age and completed an approved electrical apprenticeship with a minimum period of 5 years on licensed high/medium voltage or mains operated equipment. Approaching my twentieth year the wheels were turning.

> *Event: In November 1963, John Fredrick Kennedy is assassinated in Texas, USA.*

The jewel within

Although the workshops were named for Newport, the shops were located in the municipality of Hobson's Bay. A 15-minute walk or a short drive brought you to The Strand at Williamstown and the

Ferguson Street Pier. This was the mooring point for many of the Hobson Bay yacht club and the various bird life of the area. A world away from Jolimont and the muddy Yarra and some relief from the dust and grime of the stabling and running roads. Daily, as jobs or circumstances moved me around this city within a city, Newport workshops unfolded as the jewel in the crown.

Out of sight to the operating branches and trains running, it was the manufacturing and heavy maintenance centre of the industry. The workshops were reported to be contained in an area of about 130 acres (53 odd hectares) with buildings occupying about a sixth of its total, and a network of tracks spread over the site. The major sections of the workshops were divided into the West Block for heavy engineering and carriage building and the East Block for carriage and wagon work, including paint.

View of a section of the heritage-listed West Block (2020)

NEWPORT WORKSHOPS – THE CITY WITHIN A CITY

Each building could be identified by either work function or activity such as the foundry, pattern shop, wheel shop, machine shop, paint shop and the tarpaulin shop. Other functions within these walls were the testing laboratory under the Engineer of Tests and local shunters. Located adjacent to the North Williamstown Station was the erecting/construction shop where at different times carriage types, wagons and bridge girder sections were built and assembled. My initial experience at their door was an assault on the senses; the noise of rattle guns, the smell of burning coke and red-hot rivets, add arc flashes and it made an imagined journey to the gates of hades. The scale of this industry was far removed from my previous experiences.

Under the heading, 'Rolling Stock' the *VR Newsletter* of August 1964 reports:

> *The following new Rolling Stock was built in Department workshops during the year. (Newport, Ballarat & Bendigo) Harris suburban trailer carriages – 20, VAM twinette sleeping carriage – 1, Rail tractor – 1, Brake vans, (for freight service) -15, ALX wagons (motor cars) – 11, ELX (open wagons, general merchandise) – 24, JX wagons (bulk cement) – 20, SBX wagons (plasterboard) 5, TVF wagons (twin flex vans) – 5, VLF louver vans (general merchandise) – 29, VHX high-capacity louver vans (general merchandise) – 9, Service stock (vans and wagons for departmental traffic) – 2*

That year passed relatively quickly with the 50-cycle conversion program the major experience. Once more my electrical theory subjects were satisfactory passes but again nothing stood out. Within the shop I was possibly acknowledged as conservative, self-reliant and basically competent. Settling in over this long year had seen the odd pranks and disagreements between others, once more driven by the pay packet. Overtime was available to a core group who carried the load in both the conversion program and maintenance. Saturday morning at time and a half added to the pot and weekends at double time were fought over vigorously, although, not for third year apprentices. In some instances, Saturday mornings or the weekends was the only time that operating equipment (e.g. overhead cranes) could have major works or motors changed or electrical power services isolated. The nature of heavy industry and carriage building necessitated the imperative of overhead cranes in almost every workshop.

Yet there were other mechanisms to increase the size of the take-home pay by various allowances. All naturally inspected and appropriately approved, height allowance, dirty work allowance, confinement space allowance and many more were part of the squeeze. Nothing more entertaining than taking the production engineer up a ladder to knock grime and bird shit over him and the location. Knowing the game, he came prepared. Other benefits should be acknowledged as together with the rest of the workforce my conditions of employment included a superannuation scheme, generous sick/illness provisions and quarter fare rail tickets. Added to these employee benefits safety boots were made available at cost. They could be purchased through the stores system, form G253 at 2 pounds 15 shillings (about $5) a pair and were part of an initiative to minimise lost time injury incidents. A program of slips, trips and falls to highlight workplace safety were prominent at Newport. The business of safety and time loss days were front and centre and displayed on a large board adjacent to the administration centre.

Not on my playlist

I readily accepted the local frivolity, such as sending a lad for a population key and the occasional smallest apprentice being locked in a locker. The act of lighthearted buggery, or as they referred to it, a daisy chain or simulated doggy-style sex amusement was not on my playlist. Woe beholds the innocent inadvertently who bent over a workbench or similar. In no time a few smirking men were nose to tail … nose to tail, grinning and laughing in this choreographed dance. It seemed to be a plant shop thing and out of sight or ignored by the office. My only experience at someone's attempt concluded with me swinging a hammer and taking out the door glass insert as he ran for his pride. It was a simple message for personal space and privacy.

Yet there had been times when I provided the humour. On occasions after a mid-week function, I had nodded off on the shops train at the garden platform. A regular occurrence for a few and most times rescued by a passing well-wisher. On this occasion ignored in pleasant slumber I awoke as the train was shunted into the yard. So much for my travelling companions and workmates who clapped as I belatedly entered the shop. Much was to occur in the years ahead before the rules of workplace behaviour and welfare became law. During this period the plant shop population was relatively stable and only varied with the odd retirement and as other apprentices began to trickle in or move on. Among them were the first crop who had commenced in the manual training system. Yet it remained a mystery as to how I had missed this first-year process through the ETC and commenced at RMIT.

Historically, the training of apprentices was a Rolling Stock Branch function albeit under the direction of an Apprentice Advisory Board. This board was overseen by nominated Branch or Assistant

Branch Heads. Who or what body instituted the training centres based on skills was above my pay rate and I suspect a response to wider industry concerns?

From a note in the *VR Newsletter*, 1963:

> *The apprentice spends the whole of his first year between the training centre and the college while the three trades with most apprentices will be given manual training in their second and third year.*

The skill centre for electrical apprentices had been located in the West Block and commenced in the same year the new Railway College had opened in the 1961/62 period. The site of the original college, indiscreetly called 'bone head college' had been within the most northern boundary and close to the Newport Station. The construction of the road viaduct linking Melbourne Road to Williamstown necessitated its relocation. The hands-on skills program at the ETC were led by Senior Instructor SE Curwood, and instructors J Mitchell and NT Emmett. Other centres for car builders and boilermaker apprentices were located near at hand to their primary work role, the car shop and the erecting shop.

In September of 1964 I had a passing interest in the events occurring in far off South-East Asia. The rumour of increased involvement of Australian armed forces in Vietnam was reported in the local *Herald*, and two months later, in November of 1964, the Menzies Government introduced the National Service Scheme that required males attaining the age of 20 to register with the Department of Labour and National Services (DLNS) to enrol for the national ballot. Conscription was now legal in Australia. Win some, lose some, so by the accident of my birthdate and year I was not to be part of the lottery system.

Most of the following year I had stints in maintenance by working with others in breakdown and cyclic maintenance. With Alex Kelso on overhead crane maintenance and John Richards at the wheel shop section, the learning curve continued. This involved a wider experience and knowledge of the workshop layouts and the interaction with machine operatives and area supervisors, initially under the direction of Ron Feigan (sub-foreman) who was visible at some point in time at every location. Ron was the driver of service quality long before it was fashionable and always concerned in minimising downtime in production areas or manufacture. Tallish and lithe, his dustcoat flying as he dismounted from the shop bike, he would appear to question time lines and progress. The distance from the plant shop to the outer shops was something of a route march so supervisors of different ilk frequently used peddle power.

Examples of production are readily brought to mind with the foundry overhead cranes and the material skips. The foundry played an important role in the manufacture of brake blocks and other cast iron fittings. Non-ferrous pours were also an important but secondary function. The two cupolas were operated on a day about sequence for major pours. This enabled the lining of fire bricks to be replaced or repaired from the previous day's pour. If either the skip or cranes were immobilised due to a breakdown or unavailable during a pour it could lead to major production losses. We always responded quickly to a call from the foundry.

About this time, I was approached to join a union, with the option of the ARU (Australian Railway Union) or the ETU (Electrical Trade Union). Within the plant shop the split was about 50/50 based on age and licence qualifications. Wider counsel suggested that the ETU with national industry coverage might be more prudent. I joined the ETU.

Independent work

Independent work was the next learning phase when teamed with another apprentice. My partner was Len Hanrahan who was the opposite to me. We were easily discernible by my 181 cm to his 168 cm and my light-middle weight to his bantam weight, yet sharing some common factors, both born in Ballarat and with an odd sense of humour. Len was the a-typical country apprentice who boarded in town and returned home for the weekends to work on his beloved MG TC. He could at a moment's enquiry state the sequence of meals that were provide each night and never varied. As I recalled from my first day the majority of apprentices were selected from the regional locations. Len who had attained his driving licence immediately at age 18 was driving a 1948 Peugeot 203 and this provided the options of the occasional meal time distractions. In fairness, his attention, energy and spare time was solely devoted to rebuilding his highly-tuned sports MG. My own licence and car ownership were still years away.

Our early roles were all basic light and power 240-volt circuit installation in offices and lighting in various other settings. Memorable among them was replacing the older incandescent lamps with fluorescent lighting in sections of the canteen and adjacent storage areas. In this period the canteen provided hot meals and was set up along the lines of city location cafeterias. Business was brisk and a large proportion of the workforce ate well. For many seeking an alternative on paydays the lunch time exodus to the Railway Hotel at North Williamstown was normal.

We worked well together and had completed the circuitry with the relatively new TPS cable (thermoplastic-sheathed) replacing the rubber insulated cotton sheathed cable of yesteryears and older split conduit. Technology and products were undergoing rapid change in the field of electrical and electronics and materials for the electrical industry was not left out. Valves were replaced by transistors and solid-state diodes used in motor control.

Watch your step

Although it was relatively hot in the recess of the ceiling, we had clipped all our cable and started positioning the fluorescent fittings. Len was in the ceiling and was about to feed the cable down to be connected. I was below standing on a stepladder having screwed the fitting in place. Our drama commenced with a solid crack and a sort of cry of disbelief as Len's foot suddenly appearing through the plaster, then the other. He hung on for dear life as we secured the situation and rescue. He had overbalanced and lost his footing on the bearers and ceiling supports. A day later, with the ceiling sheet replaced, we lighted up for our first independent circuit in the glare of the white light of the fluorescents. Len and I were to team up in various other work sites and work types and share many other adventures.

Modus operandi

Each team or tradesmen involved in circuit installation was issued with a portable bench. Think; the size of a large student desk on wheels, reinforce the top surface and at one end fit a pipe vice, and at its centre, a 4-inch (100mm) jaw bench vice. Add a secure drawer and this is the base of our modus operandi as we continued to upskill. The other material/personnel carrier at hand was unique to Newport. The plant shop had battery trucks that resembled a modern golf buggy with a flatbed tray. These units enabled heavy items and motors to be moved easily and quickly to most parts of the shops. Easy to drive, with a central arm replacing a steering wheel and foot-controlled power, they provided as much entertainment as transport.

Ladders had become a normal part of our working life and I had now mastered carrying and operating a 13-foot extension ladder (before extension about 8 feet in length). At the time, ladders designated for electrical work were made of wood with a rope pull system for extension. Safety feet were not the norm and use of fiberglass not yet available. We all learnt by 'monkey see monkey do' without the benefit of national guidelines or practical instructions.

Other skills were learnt on the job including bending offset sections of conduit and transferring a tool or object from ground level to your partner on high … it's called a toss. By the book, an individual might lower a light rope to attach a hammer, a bag of clips or a pipe wrench, anything to lessen the frequency of up and down the ladder, but that is time consuming. An example might follow this sequence. Len on one ladder, me on another separated by a conduit length, as one feeds cables through, the other pulls them through. This process would be repeated as each conduit length is screwed and secured as part of the mechanical cover to the cables. Once on the ladder you learnt to bounce a metre or two either way to save repositioning and the repeatable down and up sequence. On this particular job at mid-point, Len asked for a small hammer to be tossed to him. Dually asked, dually received but with the throw a little wide of my partner's hand the hammer disappeared. Unfortunately, it landed on a glass top display case with shattering impact.

Ladders were to bring about another self-inflicted minor disaster. Once more this team were installing a watchman's security light which required an aerial connection from the back of the plant shop to the famed water tower near the Champion Road exit/entrance. Rising above the line of the distant clock tower, the water tower's design is circular and sits above several storeys of a stores section. The lower three quarters to about 10 metres are brick outer-casing with the steel water tank sitting atop. To fix the aerial connection I had positioned a ladder on the rounded surface and after drilling the fixing holes bounced the ladder to another position. Obviously because of the surface I could not tie the ladder off and Len had momentarily moved from 'footing' the ladder. Gravity and other factors came together as the ladder slipped out at the feet and I rode the 'horse' to the ground. Totally out of control as to have both hands free I had interlocked one leg through the rungs while standing on the next lower rung. Fortunately, I survived without personal damage, so too the ladder and associated equipment. Unfortunately for me we had gathered a crowd, so to a cheer and much clapping we ended the day. The following morning with yesterday's crowd absent, we finished in virtual silence.

Beyond the Newport shops

Without regular access to the *VR Newsletter*, the workforce at Newport were far from Head Office and operational announcements. Public media via *The Herald* and *The Age* were our usual source. Beyond the shops' fence line, decisions at Spring Street continued development of rail infrastructure and operational changes within the city centre. Who could have envisioned that some of these events would provide environments and links in aspects of my future working life. The new Spencer Street Terminal/Station had been opened with increased customer amenities, a café/restaurant, a train information board and the lengthening of No.1 platform to accommodate the Sydney–Melbourne interstate services.

The City of Melbourne Underground Railway Construction Branch had requested the Mines Department to commence test bores for soil/rock formations at various locations, including Flagstaff Gardens, Exhibition Gardens and another at the apex of Wellington Parade and Brunton avenue to 76 feet (15 metres).

At year's end, the *VR newsletter* item reported, 'The Manager of NWS, Mr R Roach was farewelled on his retirement by the CME WO Galletly and employees.'

The results from RMIT confirmed satisfactory pass mark in both Motor Maintenance Theory & Practice subjects. With my trade theory subjects passed, my eligibility for an A grade licence only required continuous work in SEC recognised electrical installations. The final year of my apprenticeship lay ahead. Four years had passed quickly and many locations and faces added to the roll call. My transfer indicated that I was to report to the Light & Power supervisor at Batman Avenue. Included with my transfer was the G.144 memo confirmation of my change of pay rate and the annual update of annual leave.

CHAPTER 5

THE ELECTRICAL ENGINEERING BRANCH – FLINDERS STREET

Once more I arrived at another destination better prepared in the trade and better prepared for change. I had once again ceased to be a train traveller but continued by tram. My previous memory of Batman Avenue was the flight to Jolimont workshops, now my destination was a five-minute stroll from Princes Bridge. In recent years with the relocation of the VR garage, the EE Branch had consolidated their office and a new Power Operations (PO) room. Its function recorded in the *VR Newsletter* October 1964, was to 'control and monitor the SEC 22,000-volt supply and the rail 1500-volt DC signal system'. The PO operatives visual control panel overseas the entire suburban substations and electrical supply systems.

With an exchange of paperwork and a brief chat, I was handed over to the leading hand, Barry Ely. He explained that I would be working in the Flinders Street Station (FSS) section and their priority was the Princes Gate development. I had also missed the official opening by Premier Bolte in June of last year, but other platforms and electrical installations were in plan. We proceeded via the crew paths that led to the east end of the station and over the concourse to Platform 1. At this time, many years before future successive governments were to change this precinct of the city, the east end of the platforms ended under the overhang of St Kilda Road. Today, although streamlined and modernised, the platform layout with some exceptions remains the same, albeit fully covered by Federation Square. (Notably missing the Port Melbourne and St Kilda lines converted to light rail.) Platforms 2 & 3 service the Lilydale and Belgrave lines, 4 & 5 the St Albans, Upfield and Glen Waverly lines and some Alamein services. Platforms 6 & 7 served the Dandenong line and General Motors shifts and the Frankston and Williamstown lines services. There were also through services to the Altona and Newport Workshops at peak times. Platforms 8 & 9 were for the Sandringham and Broadmeadows lines and 10 & 11 for the Port Melbourne and St Kilda services. Platform 1 centre was utilised for race and showground specials as well as the *Gippslander* train departures and arrivals. Platform 1 west, referred to as the milk dock, was dedicated to parcel traffic. The Epping and Hurstbridge services ran from two platforms at Princes Bridge and this was the site of the major building project and transformation to the new Princes Gate. The design incorporated two 18-storey tower buildings with car parks and a concrete arcade. The platform design is 10 ft (3 meters) lower than the present level for the services via Clifton Hill.

Happenings: January 1965 and platform No.13 is opened by Premier Bolte. Further west in full ceremonial mode, Engine K188 pulled down the front wall of the North Melbourne Locomotive Depot. (February 1965)

THE ELECTRICAL ENGINEERING BRANCH – FLINDERS STREET

Billeted in a box

To my surprise, the first image confronting me was my new amenities block in the dimness of the bridge overhang, a large dated portable building about 10 m x 3.5 m. Beyond the doorway was a meal table and lockers down each side for about 10 individuals, and yes it included a hand basin and running water. The standard pie warmer and urn shared the end shelf … this was to be home. Physically located beneath the station abutments for the Princes Street bridge on the through platform connecting Princes Bridge station to Flinders Street Station, undoubtably this set up was construction site logic, and yet another environment to adapt to. Straining the grey matter and to my best recollection, Platform 1 was the Gippsland departure and arrival platform.

The abutment Princes bridge, site of the past amenities (2021)

It was explained that our work ranged wide and far within the FSS precinct and the immediate surround of the train crew amenities and offices. The ERD (Electric Running Depot) was contained between the PO building and the Olympic swimming pool. This location was a hive of movement as suburban train crews came and went off and on shift.

Once more as an onlooker I was to observe the separation of roles and status. I had experienced the demarcation between trades that was as locked into awards and agreements as it was in operational crews. Separated by the length of their train this paradigm continued within the depot facilities and the amenities rooms. Drivers at one end and guards at the other.

To work again

Our priority was to undertake temporary lighting and power circuits required for station work as stages of the Princes Gate project progressed. My partner for the majority of the next 12 months was Bill Howard, an ex-New Zealander with previous experience in the commercial building industry. Bill, who in past years held a contractor's licence, sagely remarked that the term, 'wire jerker' was commonly used by the building industry for an electrician and the variety of work in this section would be less than at Newport Shops. He was spot on. Where the work at Newport needed a portable bench and a wide range of pipe wrenches and spanners, now a 'wire jerkers' kit made the grade; knife, pliers and side cutters along with an all-purpose hammer was sufficient. On being gifted a large leather tool bag I settled in to the needs of the Electrical Engineering Branch. Unperturbed, my goals were coming together as all my work would be recorded towards a licence and weekend overtime was readily available.

Some benefits were quickly recognised with my transfer to Batman Avenue. My journey trip had been halved without the extra time to Newport and the city was at my doorstep. Once more in familiar CBD territory, I was savvy with every laneway and thoroughfare from Flinders Street, north to Latrobe Street and the College. Port Phillip Arcade, Manchester Lane, Union Lane, Tattersalls Lane and via Myers, every short cut, cheap eats and toilet amenities had long been committed to memory. All feeders between the station and RMIT. Although my trade subjects were completed, I had enrolled to continue my connection to RMIT. Two subjects would complete the Supervision Certificate, my next area of interest was Electrical Contracting & Estimating. Once more the scene was set for the routine of business. The year passed rapidly with our activities revolving around electrical installations more in line with building and offices. Our work life could be hanging off ladders, steps or the occasional portable work platforms. Additional power points in offices and lighting upgrades to fluorescent units became bread and butter activities.

Flinders Street Station

The station building which had previously been little more than a transient point to and from Newport now took on a larger significance. This icon of Melbourne became a demanding child as requests for lamp replacements in platform information boards and equipment failures were everyday occurrences. Its presence is captured in the space between the Yarra River and the length of Flinders Street to Elizabeth Street. Within its dome overlooking St Paul's Cathedral is a building housing three levels at the Swanston Street end and four at the Elizabeth Street end. This is due to the gradient fall between Swanston and Elizabeth Street.

The concourse level sits above the platform levels at the eastern end to enable an overview of all trains and platform control via its multi positioned east-west platforms. Level one combined the administration and station management. Level two combined functions of the VRI (Victorian Railway Institute) including safe working classes, billiard rooms, a members' gym and the VRI library. Level three rooms were mainly used as lecture/training rooms and for operational and safe work inspectors. These upper levels were far removed from their heydays when the ballroom was a Saturday night dance constant rivalling Leggett's and the Town Hall. All had been lost in the passing years, including the building providing an open-air playground and creche. During this period, I had joined the VRI (Victorian Railway Institute) and commenced regular visits to the library.

The VRI, another independent city

Buoyed by the thousands of members and its members' services, the VRI challenged the organisation in its viability. With its statewide reach and centres in major locations it provided a social and learning glue for many employees, both male and female. Examples of its social diversity are listed in pages of the VR newsletters. These include the VRI football league with teams representing Newport W/S, Locomotive Depot, and the Suburban lines among them. They ran a Country Lightning Premiership between Ararat/Dimboola, Maryborough and Hamilton. Other sporting programs including inter-rail competitions were table tennis, fencing, golf and cricket. The *VRI Whisperer* noted the ballroom hosted the Railway Ball attended by 1200, including members from Ballarat, Bendigo, Warragul and Geelong. Manna for those employees with sporting prowess, including a little interstate travel.

THE ELECTRICAL ENGINEERING BRANCH – FLINDERS STREET

What came over you?

I was, in a way, paraded before the foreman on a misconduct charge. Unlike Edward Woodward, whose depiction of Breaker Morant in the film of his trial as he was marched before the commission left, right, left, right, left, attention, I was asked to attend accompanied by my leading hand Barry Ely. My story was simple. Over a period of some weeks our little amenities area tucked under the bridge had become unacceptable from the point of cleanliness. I had previously advised that this was unhygienic and suggested the MCC health department should be contacted. Granted one of the labourers cleaned once a day and emptied the bins but the presence of rats was visible. Unfortunately, a few of the local older apprentices continued to throw food scraps about and when requested to clean up their mess reacted poorly. Like, 'Piss off Denman, you are just on loan.'

Normally I fitted in comfortably with most groups and over a meal break would combine cards and the occasional chess game. Stepping away from my preferred persona of listen and watch, on this particular occasion I suggested. 'If you wouldn't do it at home, don't fucking do it here.' The response was a swinging fist at my head which was avoided as my combatant (let's call him Peter) overbalanced and was caught in a headlock. I might have walked him into a locker before we both crashed through the doorway before being separated. Nothing more occurred as we returned to our separate corners, I ignoring the vitriol. As detailed, my excuse was not all that well appreciated by our foreman. He was not happy and suggested that he would consider returning me to my branch. So be it. By week's end my combatant was relocated to another section and my stay at the Electrical Engineering Branch continued. The place was cleaner and the rats were under control. Bill and I had set up a 240-volt open wire trap that fried them overnight. The potential of fire was never considered at the time but it did the job.

Later in the year and my majority was celebrated with my 21st birthday and eligibility to vote. It was one of a few times where Bill and I shared a drink at Young & Jackson hotel with an extended lunch hour. The year had passed quickly and been highly profitable in terms of money earned. Among another lesson learned was that for the daily paid employee, a reasonable earning was achievable but at the expense of his social or family life. Not so profitable in terms of time, yet with overtime freely available … reap the hay while the sun shines, as goes the old saying. Yet still, I managed a hectic and busy social life that ran parallel to my working life without any crossover.

Done and dusted

On reflection, the final year of my time in the EE branch and apprenticeship passed in endless periods of six-day working weeks with the occasional seven. Money was to be made and overtime abundant. My link with RMIT was to continue with a credit pass in Electrical Contracting and Estimating. Add my first aid certificate and all that stood between my application for an A grade licence was 'practical time' on licensed work. The skyline east of the new Princes Gate was changing as the two multi-storey towers soared skyward, later to be known as the Gas & Fuel towers. During this year I had witnessed major periods of the station precinct completion from its doorstep and the images from the passing No. 48 tram. One more cog of this huge bureaucracy had been opened and explored and still more was to be revealed. I was soon to be transferred back to the Rolling Stock Branch.

THE ELECTRICAL ENGINEERING BRANCH – FLINDERS STREET

Railroaded definition: to force something to happen to someone or force someone to do something, especially quickly or unfairly.

A stuff up surely? You've got to be joking? Surely my report to memorandum was incorrect. 'You are to report to the office of the Train Lighting Inspector on Monday morning at 0800 hours.' Clearly someone was playing a joke at my expense with two years of medium/high voltage work for approval by the SEC (State Electrical Commission) outstanding. Not so. Once more this small wheel took stead and arrived at the depot's door. Included in my paperwork was my classification as an electrical mechanic. Two years absence from this location had seen large changes in infrastructure but little variation in the main focus of the depot. It was January of 1966 and my relocation was lost in the press release of the Prime Minister, Robert Menzies retirement and handover to Harold Holt. With my majority (21) behind me, I was now eligible to vote in any coming elections so I had a heightening interest in the world of politics. On a larger scale, the far-off war in Vietnam was brought into sharper focus with a younger cousin captured by the ballot.

Request for transfer

From day one, my resolution to complete the practical component for a SEC A grade licence was declared in writing, with a memo forwarded to the CME stating reasons and rationale. Response … 'Thank you but your services are required at your location.' A second memo to the CME stating reasons and rationale. Response … 'Thank you but your services are required at your location.' Repeat … repeat … repeat. Once more my priorities became second in news, cast into shadows by the approach of 'C Day'.

For a period of months, the Australian population had been persuaded by the benefits of decimalisation of our monitory system. Soon the penny of the yesterday was relegated to collectors' prizes. 14 February 1966 ... 'Australia woke to a brand-new currency.' The awkward shillings and pence derived from the British system was replaced by decimal currency, the Australian dollar.

To work again

Through this period of several months, maybe longer, the business of train inspection and servicing continued. I worked with several teams as part of the depot's non-rostered travelling workforce. In the mad house of station and platform staff, patrolling police, luggage attendants, conductors, cleaning staff and train crews we glided through the controlled confusion. The redevelopment of Spencer Street Station in 1963 had added much to the surrounds including a bus interchange and taxi ranks opposite Platform 1 as well as a specialised luggage collection point in the model of an international airport. Access to the platforms were now better managed and policed and designated as ticket only access. The other benefits in the station precinct was clearer timetable and destination information including the man in grey (station staff permanently manning this booth). Add the restaurant and a mezzanine bar and the location bustled at peak periods.

The arrival and departure of the interstate trains became my/our major day preoccupation. The Sydney–Melbourne *Inter-Capital Daylight* with its power van and travelling electrician departed Platform 1 at 0830. The set up and wave off of this train was priority one before the arrival of The *Overland* from Adelaide at 0840 on Platform 2. This train and its long distinctive all-steel carriages now took on a special significance beyond my role as a

THE ELECTRICAL ENGINEERING BRANCH – FLINDERS STREET

maintenance provider. My first interstate rail trip was to Adelaide, accompanying a recently engaged friend to a beauty from South Australia. It was to be an all-night adventure with little sleep as passengers arrived, some with brown paper parcels secreted in kit bags and carry-on luggage. The internals were comfortable bench type seating with a lower and upper bunk, set up on call by the conductor. A combination wash basin and toilet conclude the twinette internals. Breakfast was served in your suite and shoes cleaned if left in the access cubby. A last selling point may have been the declaration of air-conditioning, an established point of comfort of interstate travel and still unavailable in the suburban fleets' Harris sets. After labouring up the Ingliston Bank (1:48 Grade) the arrival at the Ballarat platform quickly became the charge of the light brigade as passengers literally ran to the catering area and the bar … last chance for a legal drink as the consumption of liquor was still a bylaw offence. From the comfort of our twinette I raised a glass to this madding crowd as a deal had been done with our conductor. Nothing like seeing the other side of the coin to appreciate the view of a customer.

Next in line was the *Southern Aurora* that had powered through the night to reach Spencer Street Station around 0900. It was a high-volume confluence of passengers seeking taxis and baggage being shipped to the luggage room or pick-up points. Overseeing the electrical staff for trains arrival/departures were two supervisors who worked a rewardable twelve-day roster of six morning and six afternoons (shift penalties plus late running swelled the coffers). Ralph Chettle and his opposite shift supervisor were mainly responsible for my engagement in these busy times and insight into the power vans operation and supply control. The business of interstate and country train running and maintenance cycles slowly became the norm as the work at Flinders Street and Princes Gate faded. So too the suburban system, that was seen only in passing from the seat of my local tram. The routine of work might be said to revolve around the Spencer Street and South Dynon carriage precincts more than the depot.

Once more the tale continued with my ongoing correspondence for a transfer. If not, a weekly occurrence it was regular and always underplayed with the benefits to both parties. Memo sent to the CME stating reasons and rationale. Response ... 'Thank you, but your services are required at your location.' Memo to CMO stating reasons and rationale. Response ... 'Thank you but your services are required at your location and no further correspondence will be entered into.' Memo to the CME stating reasons and rationale ...

My victory celebration occurred on a Friday at the Spencer Hotel with a few beers. The Spencer Hotel was the watering hole for many of the local workforce especially on a Friday night. It was my baptism of fire a year earlier when I foolishly agreed to a quick drink. Always a social drinker I was unprepared for the practice of a last round nearing six. Suddenly three beers were placed in front of me with a loud voice in the background shouting, 'time gentlemen please'. A minimum of 20 minutes to consume this lot as both the Salvos and constabulary shaded the door. Needless to say, I awoke at the North Balwyn tram terminus having napped for the previous 40 minutes. On 1 February 1966, the Licensing Act was altered to enable 10 o'clock closing with the introduction of .05 breath testing for motorists. The pace was welcome as the days of the swill were left behind.

Notice of transfer: Please report to the Chief Clerk at Newport and onto the Plant Engineer at the Plant Shop.

CHAPTER 6

RETURN TO NEWPORT – DOORS ARE OPENING

My second stint at Newport workshops was in many ways the opening door in the trade. With my 21st behind me I was starting to fall into life's pattern and a degree of stability. Much had happened in the period of my departure with the 50-cycle program extending across all of the workshops. Consider every location light and machine, powered or driven by an electric source required replacement. A new 22KV substation was in situ and a ring system of connecting switching enabled alternative feeds throughout the shops. The demise of 25-cycle supply to the 'shops' was in step with the steam locomotive.

A train traveller once more

My daily tram journey to the city via FSS continued my fleeting association with the Princes Gate project. In the months since returning to the Rolling Stock Branch the plaza over the station and east side platforms was nearing completion and the two towers heading skyward. So, with PG left behind and armed with my quarter fare ticket, my return via the workshops train was to the garden platform. Garden by name and garden by design it sat to the east side of the platform containing the first aid centre and a possibly 20-metre diameter lily pond nearest to the clock tower. Although the Harris trains were continuing to replace the older Tait variety, the shops trains remained mostly the slide door alternative. Air-flow conditional of open windows or not. Noticeably, the older core of workers had their 'own' carriage and seat position but my decision was not about a seat position: it was a non-smoker carriage. Regardless of the wipe down or cleaning process, a smoking compartment was just that; even for me as a light smoker it was tobacco entrenched.

Entering the shop was not so dissimilar to my departure some 15 months earlier, unobtrusive, the occasional handshake and welcome as I settled back in. Jim Riley and Ron Feigan still oversaw the core group of electrical staff and most faces were unchanged. Added to the roster of Alf Pugh, Alec Kelso, John Richards and others were recently qualified or soon to be qualified tradesmen including myself, Graeme Copeland and Owen Waldie. An influx of younger apprentices matched our numbers as the organisation still raised about 100 apprentices of all grades each year.

RETURN TO NEWPORT – DOORS ARE OPENING

Little has changed

Early observations confirmed that the environment of the plant shop was pretty much unchanged … the work cycle and most of the teams had their designated roles and seasons dictated the social commentary. The summer months dominated by shield cricket and why the selectors had a set against the Victorian eleven. Winter time was Collingwood, who as the workforce confirmed, were the team they loved to hate. The VFL was the biggest game in town and a few champions part of the Newport Shops, one among them, Richmond captain and VR plumber, Roger Dean.

During this early period, I was asked to become the ETU representative as the former moved on. It was possibly the case of volunteers step forward and everyone else stepping back leaving me in the glare of acceptance. The role was fairly innocuous and in the main required canvassing new apprentices or employees to join the ETU and collecting fees/dues as required. Other minor roles were in coordination with the other carriage electrician ETU rep where issues were to be brought before the 'Workshop Safety Committee'. This opportunity although not idealistically driven sat easily within my concept of social reform in the industry and fair play. Testing the memory during these times any Union Official seeking access to members during a lunch time break required an authorised invite. Their visits were mainly PR and my role to gather the sheep and provide the venue. In our case a few isolated tables. This role with the ETU soon led me to the northern sector of the city and Trades Hall. 'While you are here,' said an organiser, 'let's introduce you to our Secretary Mr Ted Innis.' A busy man, we exchanged pleasantries as I paid in the members contributions and took in the ETU's history. Ted to continue with his role in the ETU and State Labour Party and much later in the Whitlam government as I pushed ever closer to my A grade licence eligibility. One job paid my wages and the other a role of interest.

Reality quickly settled in and with a sidekick and apprentice we commenced varying roles. Whether good practice (safety would say yes) or some predetermined local agreement that I never queried, the work unit in the plant shop usually paired a tradesman with a trades assistant and an apprentice if available. Frank Filippe was to become a constant in the many months ahead. A traditional Italian, brown skinned and gregarious, Frank was employed as a tradesman assistant although his skills ranged far beyond this role from house renovation to private concreting and brickwork. Could this confirm the rumours of the honey-pot at Newport and wider skills … time would tell. He also made the best quality grappa home brew which he constantly shared in social settings. And social this younger group had become, with the fortnightly payday celebrated with a counter-lunch at the local hotels or a get together at the downstairs bar at Hosie's Hotel at 1 Elizabeth Street. The occasional after work beer in the city suited me so I joined the queue. The downstairs bar at Hosie's Hotel became the watering hole.

Family tragedy

In mid-April 1966, my father died of a severe heart attack. Beyond personal grief the system of the day provided three days bereavement leave to which I was forever grateful. Between the local administration and advice of Jim Riley the family took its time to mourn before I returned to work. Other issues beyond personal grief now came into play. Now eligible to vote my first opportunity occurred at the month's end with the new state election called for April 29. Regrettably the Bolte government was returned albeit with a smaller majority. How my political views were being shaped was surely those many milliards' factors of family economics, customs and environment. My social consciousness in justice and opportunity was being honed and undoubtably looking from inside the workshops to the wider world was another perspective. The shadow of Menzies at the federal level (1949–66) and Bolte at state level (1955–72) was all my generation and some prior generations had known. It fitted that beautifully illustrated option of vanilla or chocolate; take one or the other, yet the choice excluded those many other flavours and the two levels of Australian politics had become just that.

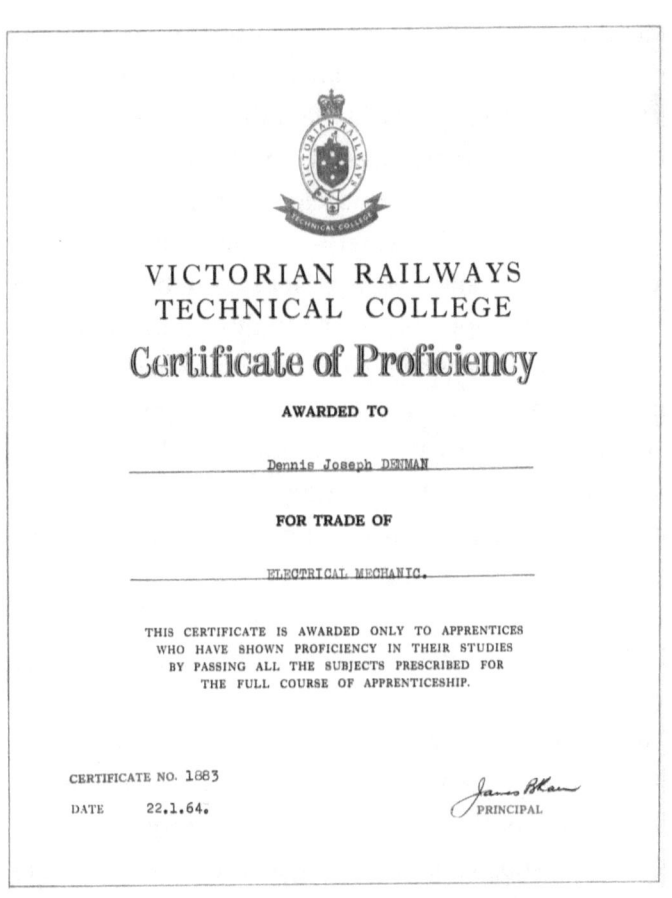

Certificate of Proficiency 1964

In this year (1966) my Certificate of Completion of Apprenticeship also arrived to formally change my status. Dennis Joseph Denman had completed his course of training as an Electric Mechanic. (No.1986) I was continuing other subjects at RMIT building on my Supervisor's Certificate. This year's unit enrolment included Legal Aspects and Principles of Management. I had additionally enrolled and attended a six-week industry safety course at South Melbourne Technical School. The safety course covered potential hazards, material handling and steps in elimination or protection.

Safety and safe practices were a conditional part of working in heavy industry and there were daily examples of near misses and incidents on my doorstep. My ladder fall was one and a procession of individuals including myself, to attend the nurse for eye conditions (always recorded as foreign body in eye) was a constant. The best of intent wearing safety spectacles only minimised the dusty conditions. In short, self-preservation, but also wanting to understand the principles of hazard analysis and reduction. Visible steps and programs were being initiated in the workplace. The slips, trips and falls initiative was being presented by Ron Jenkins the Safety Officer, who was soon to became another contact beyond Newport. The theme that managing safety is good business was front and centre. A year earlier and the *VR Newsletter* noted W (Bill) Cox, (Rolling Stock Safety Officer) and Allan Firth (Electrical Engineering Branch, Ass. Engineer-in-charge of Tests) completed the RMIT Industrial Safety & Accident Prevention course.

Again and again, the diversity of work type and social change was occurring on my watch. Within the electrical industry products and mediums were rapidly changing. Technical reps beat a passage to the doors of the shops and the next generation of apprentices were adding to the conversation of new products or options. Gone or redundant like the era of steam, the trade replaced split conduits either with solid screwed or plastic. Gone, cloth covered cabling, replaced mainly with PVC insulation and TPS. New techniques and technologies joined the mid-twentieth century. Other applications included, (MI) Mineral Insulated cable – pyro cable that was fireproof and waterproof that would soon replace external circuits in locations in the foundry and for external fuel points. Mains cabling systems of open cable trays that were interlaced in length and could replace the 3-inch (75 mm) water pipe that had normally provided the physical protection. It made the work easier and more efficient. Besides the technology, was the introduction of power and explosive tools, including nail guns that enabled fixing to concrete and steel. Among the options, the Ramset brand which could be used without a licence and in minutes replace hours of drilling and plugging bracket and clip supports. Electric motor types and control systems had also followed suit. Efficiencies and cost reduction had become an unspoken component of our work roles. There was still much to learn and more changes and wider efficiencies were in hand.

Beyond the Newport workshop's bubble, in September 1966 the *VR Newsletter* records the five-year hire of a 140-system floor computer from General Electrics (GE) Pty Ltd. A statement specifying its first job was to provide for the control and accounting for railway stores, followed by payroll preparation with later applications to freight statistics and wagon control. The *VR Newsletter* also recorded in the following month that the Minister for Transport, Mr Ray Meagher, on his return from a three-month tour said, 'Melbourne couldn't survive without an underground railway.'

Surely another politician's headline grab for a vote, so what in the hell was this MURLA? My eyes were firmly fixed to that A Grade qualification and beyond that an increasingly active social life. So, to another misquote: All work and no play makes Jack a dull boy.

Accordingly, the periods of my arrival at the garden platform asleep in the carriage increased week upon week. Returning from midweek and Friday night social engagements with only hours before work started was normal. Melbourne and my non-rail peer group could be seen at Leggett's palladium, the various suburban town halls, such as Heidelberg, Hawthorn and Moorabbin. Lakeside Power House was additionally a favourite haunt. The wider world including Australia was undergoing massive social changes, albeit the comments by actress, Ava Gardener (*On the beach*, 1959) some years prior that, 'Melbourne was the perfect place to make a film about the end of the world'.

> *Much was to occur in echoing a Bob Dylan song title, 'TheTimes They Are a-Changing'.*

There was a lot to be learned in the coming periods, as location after location was to provide variety and different opportunities for cyclic maintenance and the occasional breakdowns.

The West Block and beyond

Where instances of the past are somewhat clouded over time, the sounds of the stamping hammers hitting the red-hot axles as they were shaped and finished remains clear. This function would, like steam, soon fade and cease. Beyond this site the stores steel holding section was serviced by two outside gantry cranes. These cranes ran on ground level rails with a main single girder supported at either end by an A-type welded frame. These units were ground controlled by a single operator using a hand-held pendent station to move both the crane direction and load positioning. Long load semi-trailers could be placed beneath these gantries to enable their steel to be off-loaded to their relevant size positions. What could go wrong? Anything from motor failures to the pendent guides either broken or unclipped to wiring failure. A medley of sorts. Other stores handling equipment included a service lift between floors (general storehouse) and single electric hoists set on a H beam able to be swung through a 180-degree radius. These units were also controlled by a single operator using a hand-held pendent station. All handling and lifting equipment were regularly tested to specified load limits and all lifts carrying persons as well as stores must be tested annually by a Licenced Lift Inspector (Department of Labour regulation). Material or carriage handling was a major component of most of the East Block roads where refits and upgrades were the major roles of each section. Our role was to keep this ancillary equipment turning … small wheels but part of the big picture.

As another year began, 1967, I was back to RMIT for units in Personal Management and Statistical Methods (having passed last year's electives), as on the ground the threesome continued to be used on a variety of maintenance roles and in the ever expanding 50-cycle program. Beyond the Newport fence the many hours of overtime has been exchanged for wheels; an XR Ford Falcon 500 sedan. For years past I had the use of a friend's second vehicle but only locally and never to work, now the workplace journey had options. From this point on, true independence was mine and holiday breaks enabled the views of Sydney, Adelaide and Broken Hill to replace postcards. Though still a conforming bachelor, the chase of young women took on options beyond the metropolitan boundaries. More importantly the roads to and from Newport did not necessitate two rails. This year was to take on more meaningful propositions other than my new-found freedom.

Annual leave

The heat of summer has never been my go so where possible I had opted to work through the Christmas period shutdown. The benefits included less crowded off-peak periods. Taking the advantage of an interstate rail pass, I had opted to cross the Nullarbor on the *Transcontinental* (renamed *Indian Pacific* in 1970). Commencing from Adelaide you travelled by local to Port Augusta to join the then *Transcontinental* departing for Perth. My insight into rail operations was on the rise. Distant from leisure time, outside influences for a short time held centre stage. With Menzies' retirement, the new flag bearer for PM was Harold Holt. Holt may be remembered for many things above his loss at sea at Victoria's Cheviot beach and his 'all the way' slogan with LBJ the visiting American President. Yet he was the architect in proposing a federal referendum (27 May 1967) on two issues: one defeated and forgotten and significantly for the recognition of our indigenous Australians (Aboriginal peoples) in the Constitution and Census, a YES result by all states to 91%, and my first vote in a federal election.

Freelance, and roving commission

For the following years a combination of installation jobs and other work saw the team progress to all points of the shops. The inventory of work types and contacts had begun. Pattern makers could do this, the foundry could cast this, the turnery could face this and any welding or … the rumour of the honey pot was real. Meanwhile, the plant shop grew in numbers with characters on both sides. Notable among the fitters were Eric Barclay, Ron and Kenny, while our group numbers increased with more apprentices Kevin McPoyle, Neil and Michael, and a new tradesman, Graham Button to name a few. This wide group of personalities were to be daily entertaining and occasionally a pain, yet they provided a collegial environment. Football, football, football, it was impossible to ignore, with the day-to-day interest that demanded competitive support.

In those days, different times, the workforce looked forward to the holiday periods and any excuse for a long weekend. The odd illness report (up to five single days without a certificate) enabled the workforce much flexibility in mini absent periods. It was seen as a normal perk and rarely questioned. Simple examples are of the Show Day holiday, then on a Thursday, add one sickie; four days break, yet Melbourne Cup Day was not. For the workforce interested in racing, the day was spent organising Cup sweeps and 'en masse' returning to the shop where the race call was heard over the radio speakers.

In my other role as the local ETU representative, my visibility quietly grew with a close liaison with Frank Wegrzynowski, ETU representative for the car electrician section. Frank was proactive in many areas of safety and health issues and he used me as a double act ... strength in numbers. This position enabled closer dialogue with the supervisors in both locations in settling/discussing minor issues. Ron Milne was the Car Shop Electrician Forman. Here James Riley was a sympathetic ear. Jim as the Senior Forman was a quiet conscientious individual with a calm and engaging disposition and any issue start point. Technically competent and open to suggestions he had unknowingly become a sort of work environment mentor from the period of my father's death. Simple queries on superannuation and qualifications. Possibly his own progress had been somewhat similar. He was the Newport Workshops Foreman's Representative for the Australian Transport Officers Federation (ATOF) and involved in salary and award negotiations. Many years later random research in the *VR Newsletter* of 1976 cited the third reunion of the 1942 VR apprentice intake. The function was held at the Brunswick ballroom. In attendance, Mr J Riley, Railway Foreman, Mr W Chapman, NWS Manager and included guests of Mr G F Brown (Deputy Chairman of Commissioners) and Mr L Rolls (Superintendent of Loco Running).

In the East Block, Wheel Shop Maintenance section, I was settling in to my next location. Frank out, Maurie in as my trades assistant. Maurie was another of the mainly invisible characters at Newport. Of English heritage some of his mannerisms resembled the cartoon character Andy Capp. Yet behind this demeanour was a sharp punting brain and a roll of a thousand dollars readily found. He was more a banker than a gambler and happily accepted a 10% return. A regular race goer we occasionally passed each other when I was trackside.

The section came with a bench and test equipment behind a locked door with hot water and a telephone. Maintenance on call and every supervisor used our number without the need to go via the plant shop. We were on call for all of our shift with the benefit of 30 minutes paid time for lunch with preventative maintenance to be undertaken during the operators' lunch break ... formally a straight shift. The sections priority remained the foundry, skips and cranes. The erecting shop, carriage fabrication and conversions where the technology of welding types, Metal Inert Gas (MIG) and Gas Metal Arc Welding (GMAW) wire feed units were more in use. Technology was ever changing and present. So, too the executive team and local management. The Bolte Government had selected Mr Vernon Wilcox as the new Transport Minister. New appointments were announced for the VR commissioners with the new Chairman of Commissioners, Mr George Brown, supported by Mr E P Rogan as Deputy Chair and Mr L A Reynolds as Commissioner.

Violet Town rail accident (Feb. 1969)

The news bulletins of all the TV stations highlighted the tragedy. The following morning at every morning tea and lunch break much of the conversation was about the *Southern Aurora* disaster and the reported deaths of nine and many injuries still to be confirmed. My memory was in overdrive trying to place if the train was crewed by the Victorian Railways or New South Wales Government Rail crews. With TLD being my last location prior to Newport, this silver interstate train was one that I knew carriage by carriage. Sadly, the following days confirmed the specifics of the head-on collision and the crew fatalities. The inquiry's detailed report in July revealed that the driver of the *Southern Aurora* died of cardiac failure some time before the collision. Sweeping recommendations were to follow including duration changes (more frequent intervals) to medical examinations for drivers, trainee drivers and firemen. Another action was the modification of the vigilant control system compelling an acknowledgement by the driver or fireman within a specified period.

Front page news, Union business

Sometime during this period, a decision on relief instructors at the training centre came to the fore. Frank Wegrzynowski (Car Electrician ETU rep) approached me with his concerns that non-electrical trades (turner and fitters) were being used for absent periods, such as annual leave, extended illness and long service periods in the training centre. The position of the ETU was forwarded to the manager. After discussions with the workshop manager, it was agreed that future absent periods would utilise electrical trade staff and the senior instructor vacancy would hold an A grade licence. This resolution was local, small in context, but wider social upheaval was being orchestrated by the ACTU and the Labour party. Resistance by the community to the Vietnam War was growing and Bourke Street resounded to the voices of 100,000 anti-war demonstrators in May 1970.

Rail to road

Sometime during this period, the car became my daily work horse arriving to park outside the shops in Champion Road. Once more the benefit column had outscored the loss column in daily travel. There is no straight line between the suburb of Kew and Newport/North Williamstown but some particular routes minimised traffic and time. Kew junction via Johnson Street Collingwood was a direct line to the North of the city enabling the swing through College Crescent (north of Melbourne University) to approach Dynon Road via North Melbourne to Footscray. The journey continued by either Hyde or Whitehall streets to Yarraville and Douglas Parade to Newport and the workshops. Unknown at the time, but appreciated in later years, this journey sequence (Whitehall Street and Douglas Parade) placed me as a witness to the sites of major capital works programs for the City of Melbourne and the western suburbs. The West Gate Bridge Project commenced sometime in 1968 and a year or two later the Newport D power station controversially plagued by Trade Hall go/no go bans. The West Gate Bridge piers towering skyward above the Yarra was my daily view from behind the windscreen. Time is readily measured in conventional ways, by the hour, but also events or occurrences of special periods, an award, graduation, a birthday, holiday periods. Some to most, more to many. My time at Newport was beginning to approach a decade when the next round of supervisor's exams was advertised to be held on the 21/10/1970 and 18/11/1970. Coached by both Ron (Snowy) Milne and Jim Riley and with access to past exam papers, (I'm sure all other candidates had equal access) I somehow managed a pass.

West Gate Bridge

Regrettably, October of 1970 will be long remembered by a generation with the West Gate bridge collapse of a span between piers 10 and 11 on the western side. I had passed that construction hours before driving along Whitehall Street via Douglas parade. Thirty-five workers died and many others were injured on that fateful day. It remains Australia's worst industrial accident. The diverted drive home was of small inconvenience given the devastation and loss of life. It would take a period of community mourning, and a major investigation before a 1980 completion date.

> Memo from the Chief Mechanical Engineer's office. R.S. 70/5835
> *I have pleasure in advising that you were successful in passing the examination for appointment to supervisory positions in the electrical division. An entry to this effect has been made on your departmental history. Signed S Keane.*

CHAPTER 7

OVERALLS TO DUST COAT – A ROVING COMMISSION

The SEC gained a highly credentialed inspector when Ron Feigan resigned. John Richards took his place and I, through apparent seniority (exam date), began the cycle of relief supervisor from the Wheel Shop section. Promotion in large organisations (state bureaucracy, armed forces, state school teachers) historically held tight to the edict, 'the best qualified person for the job' with the rider of seniority if there is a need to separate to equally qualified persons. Unquestionably this was a tenet of the Victorian Railways, yet in operational and station grades, seniority came first. This was my first encounter with the rules of the day. This system produced a domino effect as advancement was then tied to vacancies from age retirement, resignation or death. Talent might be an important factor, but timing even more.

In an internet article titled, 'Platforms & Trains – Flinders & Jolimont Yard Stories', John Drake recalled his early experiences when first starting driving suburban trains in late 1972 at the ERD:

> *'I don't know about the guards' end but certainly at the drivers' end there was further demarcation. The senior drivers' table was just inside the door and was known as the six-overcoat table ... those drivers had to have at least 15 years' experience and were usually on the 'A' rosters. Woe be-tide any junior driver who dared sit at this table even on night shift when no-one else was there.'*

That year, headlines and banner leads were front and centre of TV screens and the newsprint. Some with far-reaching impact, others with less effect. On 22 August, Henry Bolte resigns and Dick Hamer is elected premier; on 5 December, the Whitlam Government is elected. At Newport workshops the recommendations of the Bland Report caused hardly a ripple, including the operation of the railways by a Board. The Victorian Railway Board replaced the VR Commissioners in December 1972. The first Hitachi suburban train begins on the St Kilda line. Melbourne's rail commuters were yet to reap the benefits of an air-conditioned train.

Sage advice

Jim Riley had given me some sage advice on notification of my exam results. Never knock back the opportunity to gain wider experience or promotion. Plan for the future and take up the offer of additional superannuation units. I did. With the other location supervisors working shift work and main holiday periods you may be transferred for periods of a minimum week to 12 weeks at a time. And income was important. Mid-1973 and the Industrial Tribunal granted an over award payment. This State Incremental Payment Scheme (SIPS) of $4.20 per week plus $15.90 for tradesmen authorised by the government. Other benefits flowed with half-fare work travel allowances reduced to quarter-fare.

> *Pack your bags: Train Lighting Depot, Jolimont Workshops, the Newport Car Electricians ... the merry-go-round began for an extended period of the next few years.*

Would you believe

Somewhere in the personnel book of dos was a fit to drive a VR vehicle requirement. Notwithstanding that I held a Victorian licence to drive a car, I was required to take the department's advanced driving test. Maybe it was an insurance or legal requirement to get it done. So, I reported for my test. A large capable individual buckled me into the seat, checked the mirrors positioning and asked me to drive north from Spencer Street. Within a number of city blocks I was requested to give a running commentary on aspects of traffic in front and around the car as well as the moving traffic sequence. Paraphrase:

> *Driving north the car in front of me is indicating left with the truck in the second lane braking to indicate a right hand turn at the next intersection. The lights are green and have been green for about 30 seconds ...*

Much later, at the extremities of the northern suburbs he demonstrated severe braking conditions and handling on an unmade road. My turn was to his satisfaction and hours later I received my tick of approval. What an adventure and the following day I drove the depot ute to South Dynon on the morning shift. TLD commenced with a 12-day unbroken shift rotation commencing on a Monday to Saturday 1.30pm–9.00pm, Sunday to Friday 6:30am–2.00 pm. Overwhelmed and out of my depth, the abilities and support of the workplace group made the daily transition progressively easier. The arrival and departure of the interstate trains were the major responsibility of the role, i.e. waving the travelling electrician off, welcoming him in. The *Southern Aurora* was docked at the station for an hour or so before its departure at 8.30pm to enable the train to be pre-heated or cooled.

There were moments

The overload breakers in the power-van were tripping out and wouldn't reset. The normal procedure was to isolate each carriage one by one to identify the fault. That sometimes meant removing the jumper leads (flexible power cables between carriages) as part of this isolation process. A second-class carriage near the rear of the train was identified so I advised the shunters of the need for a replacement carriage. What happened? The *Southern Aurora* was broken up and the carriage replaced. The train crew and shunters worked at top pace to remake the train. Hundreds of passengers were left standing on the platforms or arriving to a dislocated train. Dining car staff and conductors were stretched to capacity for services. Station staff were busy undertaking a public relations exercise. The premier flagship train had departed an hour late. Many wheels had come together to resolve the problem.

Postscript: Decision-making to that level of public scrutiny had not been part of my training but experience would/may improve that adrenalin rush and clear head.

Someone had contacted Ralph Chettle (my opposite shift supervisor) at home and he arrived within a half hour to support the new boy, me. A gesture long appreciated. Mentally exhausted, after completing my incident report, signing off at 10.00pm to commence again at 1.30pm the following day. The remuneration was great but the sleep-work turnaround cycles were hard. This was years before the call for greater work-life balance.

JWS welcomed me to take over the motor section for the short term. One glance through that aromatic smoke screen and I was reunited with Neil McMillian, now the Senior Foreman. Buster McMaster-Smith was officiating on the 'wall' while Don had taken promotion at TLD. Neil explained the role, followed by the introductions to the electrical fitters and labouring staff in the section. With the motor section located immediately adjacent the office, my role would seem to be, work allocation, problem-solving, work group interactions and with their help, learning about direct current motor refits.

Once more the feeling of inadequacy lingered at my shoulder as this role took in the gallery where the motor coils and armatures were repaired. None of my past roles other than unit (motor) exchange as a first-year apprentice was relevant to the work that was required. I was soon to learn that there were factors other than repairs. There was a 'shop's agreement' of a maximum number of refits/rebuilds of motors per day. It was a (who knows when) management/union quota system. One more oddity of the day.

A mini revolution

Surprise, surprise, there was a revolution on the floor, at least a one-man one. A fifth-year apprentice, let's call him Mick, decided to up his quota and add extra completed motors to his day's output. He worked consistently without undue haste and enjoyed the furore and uproar he created. My first union (ARU) meeting to re-establish the status quo was overseen and settled with Neil Mac and the local rep. I was now on the other side of the table in this role and was soon to question my position as an ETU representative. Mick was not impressed with the outcome but peer pressure wore him down. We were to cross paths again in the year ahead at the plant shop.

Business mixed with humour

Like a magnet, my time around Neil was ever a step from humour. Within days of my arrival, he had a minor dispute over his annual leave credits. With his dispute resolved, he turned to me to repeat his favourite mantra: *All clerks are bastards but not all bastards are clerks.* Readily explained to anyone who listened and naturally he commanded the ear of all in the office, including the junior clerk. It was about equity, a junior clerk from his first day was eligible for a first class pass with 12 months service during his holiday period. Not so the blue-collar work-grades who had to complete 20 years of service before his changed status from second class passes. It was a divide that was to change in the years ahead.

> *How Neil came to be sitting in his jocks: Caught by a hose break as a motor casing was being cleaned his suit covered in dirt, he decided to hand wash the damage. He left that evening his suit resembling an outfit of the stage comedian larrikin, Roy Rene.*

I survived with the help of all around me, supervisors and local workforce. I was also in the good books because I had ordered and distributed tools and equipment that was long overdue. Observation and information were some of my strengths. At every location I had copied the store inventory and walked the floor space of every storehouse. The store's inventory was the key to the candy store.

After a month I was relocated to the inspection shop and for the following weeks oversaw the works within the shop and external stabling yards. The decade was lost in movement and consolidation to roles. The next period was dispersed between some months back at the wheel shop section before a period at the car electricians. I was to work for/with another memorable character here, Ron Milne, a bustling, energetic and knowledgeable individual and the full bottle in the 'electrics' of the suburban and country fleet units. A man that murdered a pot and enjoyed nothing more than fishing in the bay for pinkies and anything larger. I was to enjoy a season of snapper fishing departing from his mooring in the Frankston Creek long before daylight. Much can happen in a season of fishing from small sharks taking a snapper at the gunnels edge to wind and tide combining to have us up to our knees pushing the runabout along the creek. I was additionally a suitable swabby because I never accepted a beer even on a mill pond; I was a fair-weather sailor.

Day on day, I was brought up to date as we pored over wiring diagrams to compliment the carriage program of refits and modifications. Here the work group electricians were of a mainly older cohort and worked in established teams. They were diligent, yet within a short time the blind was asked to lead the blind. On this particular day with someone unavailable (off sick) I asked, let's call him Harry, to connect the cabling underneath the carriage. To my surprise he related that he always connected the drivers cab circuitry and didn't know what occurred below deck. Fortunately, hiding a broad smile and armed with a detailed circuit diagram we were able to finalise the connections. Wiring blueprints/circuitry I could do, albeit I was just passing through.

The merry-go-round recorded in my personnel file read of a continuous period relieving as a supervisor at, Jolimont, T.L Depot, Jolimont, Newport, Jolimont, Newport, T.L. Depot Newport, Newport, T.L. Depot and Newport.

> *May 1973: Amended Railways Act 1972. Management passed from Victorian Railway Commissioners to a VR Board and to trade as VicRail.*

During most of my time at Newport I had opted to work through the Christmas period shutdown. The benefits were two-fold, work access for major works could be prioritised without any interruption to production schedules and less crowded periods. So, taking advantage of an interstate rail pass, the family was able to take the *Vinelander* to Mildura. With the benefits of the motorail service, the Volvo was unloaded at Mildura, and a magnificent sight-seeing holiday commenced.

> *Events: Mr R Meagher replaces Mr V Wilcox as Transport Minister in a cabinet reshuffle.*

Next step

My next role as a supervisor was to qualify as an Authorised High Voltage Operator. The establishment of the 22KV substations within the workshops enabled control and oversight by the Power Operation Centre at Batman Avenue. These substations were within a fenced, locked and controlled environment identified as high voltage. At times or situations, there were instances when the HV power supply had to be isolated or redirected due to faults or maintenance. Over a period of some weeks, I was trained and exposed to locations across the HV network where I could learn the protocols and operate switching under authorised control. All went well and I was duly cited with a tick.

> The memo from the Chief Electrical Engineer's office, 13 July 1973.
>
> *I hereby declare that you Mr D Denman, Plant Shop Sub-Foreman, are an authorised operator as defined in the Instructions relating to high voltage apparatus. Signed, Alan Firth.*

Once more back to the tools again before a salaried position opens. James McKinlay Riley has been promoted to Train Lighting Inspector and vacates the seat. The next initial steps were for John Richards to act as the senior foreman and the sub-foreman's vacancy to be advertised. I was to act in that capacity until …

It's certainly different. But then, so was I. By that I mean that some conventions didn't fit my persona. During my learning time as a supervisor, I had missed the mould in a number of ways. I declined to wear a tie at work, although seen by some as part of the authority dress. I had watched the demarcation line between blue and white collar from day one and this decision was about acceptance on the floor and practicability. No particular dress code was advised, just the issue of the standard grey dust coats. Regardless of the statement in fashion marketing, 'that clothes maketh the man'. Not so under a pit covered in grime and shit.

CHAPTER 8

SUB-FOREMAN – VIEW FROM THE OTHER SIDE

Slowly, slowly, in the past few years my confidence as a supervisor had steadily grown and I felt better prepared to supervise a peer group. Given the choice, my recommendation was to start at a different location, removing the element of the odd commentary that might be construed as 'not as I used to do, but do as I say'.

My entry to the plant shop office was years in the making. The timing by some events outside my control, albeit the coincidence of time and qualifications when mixed with resignations and vacant position. Promotion by seniority can be a long slow progress. Other talent had moved on and if other factors were considered, they weren't. Maturity and married life added a touch of stability, for me, yet not part of the equation. Much like my driver's licence, a long time coming.

I was now living in Ashburton and varied travel between train and car. At this time, John Kift was the Plant Engineer or OIC. He was pugnacious and short in height with a personality that exuded energy and confidence. We soon found common ground when he became aware that I had completed a supervisor's certificate and other management units at RMIT. The VR industry was proactive in bringing talent up through the ranks, exampled by the number of commencing apprentices that became linked to the scholarship programs or cadet schemes for engineering opportunities. The examples of two commissioners being part of former apprentice intakes was a publicity gem. Not as well publicised was the exit of tradesmen, around 85% on completion of their apprenticeship. The department's loss a boon for private industry. These cadet programs provided welcoming opportunities for apprentices, but similar to the foreman's grades, provided little help in man management and innovation. The days of MBAs and other commercial experience outside the rail was years away.

> *Memorandum: Electrical Mechanic D.J. Denman. I have pleasure in advising that subject to covering approval you have been selected for appointment to the position of Sub-Foreman, Class 7 at Newport Workshops. Your promotion to be effective as from 17/7/1973 with alteration of classification from Electrical Mechanic to Sub-Foreman, Class 7 at the salary prescribed for that grade, viz: $5490 per annum. Signed, S Keane CME.*

After discussions with Jim Riley, I resigned from the ETU to become a member of the Australian Transport Officers Federation.

In the preceding year the ATOF had conducted a work value case in the Commission. The resultant outcome was a restructure of the classification grades/levels and a percentage increase to the higher grades. Effectively they reversed the grade identifier and removed the bottom level. My classification grade moved from Class 7 to Class 2 with no change of remuneration. My interest in work value salary grades was piqued.

New team

Richo and I were to make a very different regime than any previous one. Different in many facets including personality. John was the action man and was sort of tethered to a rational thinker that would look for facts or information before any decision. Sometimes it helped and sometimes it might hinder, but as a team we complimented each other. Socially we got on and had run the Tan together, played golf and enjoyed a social beer. I recall earlier trade situations when paired together when we needed a welder to tack some brackets. Take a Saturday morning job and no welders available. Richo taking command and using an arc welder cascaded molten welding residue onto his upper legs in tacking our brackets. Low level burns requiring attention and a medical diagnosis. He had improved since then, but other instances were at hand.

One day we entered the HV substation compound and John approached the external 22KV disconnect switch which was operated manually. The operation required removing the lock and pulling the mechanism downward to disengage the three phase knife switches. I had entered the building housing the transformers and PO phone. The protocol was as follows. Contact the PO officer indicating my name and switch identifier and requesting permission to undertake the switching. Only when he had confirmed permission should the switching be actioned. Mid-conversation there was a roar and a flash as the switch was opened under load to create a huge arc. Seconds later the switch was rammed back as shards of molten copper fell at John's feet. Somehow or other we retrieved the switching, kept the PO officer on side and signed of the action in the record book. An isolated incident, but confirmed the rationale behind the High Voltage protocols.

He was an easy person to work for and with. Outside of work hours and many hours within, John had become possessed by horse racing and the promise of additional income. Anyone at the metropolitan Saturday meeting would hear his voice rallying a win or decrying a losing ride. His enthusiasm was engaging.

Reality confirmed

The needs of business didn't stop with the change of regime. The march of the 50-cycle program continued as the shops by locations and priorities came on line. New works required an expenditure identifier (number) to be raised against our cost centre. The stable 399601 against general work was heavily used and seemed to be an endless bucket. The units of RMIT were beginning to be of use. New faces were appearing as the apprentice stream continued to roll through the system as others completed their time. Socially, they were a different group with a few regular users of low-level social drugs. Although my generation had been saturated by cigarette advertising, social drugs played no part in my social life. Without any knowledge of marijuana use or its effects I/we were out of our depth. Probably a cop-out but it never to my knowledge became a topic within the supervisor/management group. Yet memory is sometimes elusive and surely aspects of safety were discussed. Equally we were never

SUB-FOREMAN – VIEW FROM THE OTHER SIDE

(to my memory) provided with sobriety tests/advice leaving this group of supervisors to require suspect individuals to be booked off duty. An easy out as it minimised paperwork and formal please explains. Not so in the operational grades. It would take many years before Health and Welfare Acts drove corporate policy and drug testing to became an industry norm.

Not immediately, but change also came with a new plant engineer: John Kift out and Don Furlong in. Regrettably Alex Kelso resigned for greener pastures, a valued team player lost. Don was viewed by the workforce as somewhat out of place with his fashion suits and high heeled and soled shoes. His legacy, possibly more for the tree-lined planting along Champion Road than anything else that comes to mind. I recall him walking into the office past a group of electrical staff who were at their lockers having returned early to the shop. He walked up to me and said, 'Go and tell your staff they are early and not to be back before 3:45.' So, I did. Was this an example of management authority or, why bark yourself when you have dogs to bark for you? Overthought? Maybe.

Other tales added to the folklore of the shops

A number of supervisors' bikes had been seen disappearing into the garden lily pond. Apparently, the bikes had cluttered the entrance to the clock tower so had been dispatched to their temporary grave. The manager's name was withheld.

A certain plant sub-foreman had taken his boss by car to the nearest public house after he was questioned as to the whereabouts of his workforce, name withheld. The unidentified 10 accepted the loss of pay from midday and a warning of future damage control. Some among them soon became informally known as the brothel boys.

Stories of this minor cadre soon circulated about their weekly visits and exploits. Different times and a different population made aspects of their supervision a little more challenging.

An unnamed foreman with an interest in roses, who bragged about his prowess to identify scotch was set up. At an after-hours retirement function, with two whiskeys of the same brand (Haig's) he swirled and tasted, nominated and failed. Ho, Ho.

After a minority of individuals were sprung with the odd foreigner-made items the general security of the 'shops' had been reviewed. Rumour of a couple of yards of overfill concrete redirected to a supervisor's driveway was unsustainable. A senior manager is rumoured to have been asked to resign over a trailer build. Well, that was a surprise or otherwise careless for almost every item of value was branded with the initials VR, including my arse.

Mea culpa … all of the following. Absent without leave for extended counter lunches; personal foreigners; cushion upholstery, zinc and chrome plating on various car parts; and some 21st key blanks before plating. Use of the workshops truck to bring a refrigerator onto the premises. Organising a mini tarp manufacture for home use … it's no excuse, but we were all a product of the railway culture.

Two years into my time in the office and I had been offered periods of relief at the Training Centre. Others had related to me that they, the apprentices would drive me mad and I would be on my feet most of every day. Secondly the initial role would be material filing and scrapping and not specifically circuit board work. Notwithstanding I settled in for a month to wet my feet. During this initial period the ETC was relocated to the East Block from its West Block location. I was soon to move also.

CHAPTER 8

ELECTRICAL TRAINING CENTRE – A NEW CALLING

Here we go again, a different environment where my skill set and knowledge were outside of the requirements. The Electrical Training Centre (ETC) was set up to a layout provide by the Plant Engineer's Office (Drawing code Z 2-5.5) and approved in May 1971. In total, the proposed area of the centre was 7727 sq ft (or 720 sq metres). At the time overseen by Ken Gennifer and a small group of highly skilled individuals, they had settled into an area adjacent to the office of the Superintendent of Carriage Maintenance and near the Car Builders' Training Centre.

The set up was an office and tool store with an open plan area that was divided into three independent sections. Alan Dawes ran the machine shop of lathes, pedestal drills, shapers and a few milling machines. Ron (Doc) Little coordinated and was always present in all areas used for hand tool skills. Alf Robinson ran the electrical board circuitry and motor section. In my initial times I was the swing man for hand skills and second banana to Doc. The ETC oversaw a full-time skills program for first year apprentices that utilised skills in machine and hand skill application. The end product was the manufacture of tools and models for their future trade use.

Model bogie wheel, apprentice 27, 1978

Much was to happen over the next three months. Ken (Senior Instructor) took a period of long service leave and advised of his impending retirement. This prompted a vacancy for a Manual

ELECTRICAL TRAINING CENTRE – A NEW CALLING

Training Instructor which was advertised from the Office of Workshops Manger.

Hailed as I attempted to cross the roadway on my way to the plant shop, the workshop manager pulled the car over to ask me how I was settling in. Exchanging pleasantries, I replied that next to his job, I could see apprentice training as my next step. Confirming my interest, he continued on his journey. Months later my application was one of many. I had found Les Rolls open and approachable. He was an energetic and forceful character with a playful sense of humour.

> *A redacted copy of 8 applicants, Circular 71/75*
>
> *Foreman Supervisor Mr D J Denman has been acting as a manual training instructor in the Electrical Training Centre since 2/2/75, has acted for short period prior to this and always carried out the duties satisfactorily. In addition, being a qualified electrical supervisor, he is the holder of an SEC wiring licence. The holder of such a licence is considered to be a most desirable feature for electrical trade instructor. For the above reasons, of the applicants from Newport Workshops, Mr Denman is considered the best qualified and most suited for the position, and his selection is recommended. Forwarded for your consideration.*
>
> *Signed L.C. Rolls Workshop Manager.*

> *Memorandum. RS.75/6012. Chief Mechanical Engineer's Office. 22 August 1975*
>
> *Sub-Foreman (FS2) Mr D J Denman. I have pleasure in advising that subject to covering approval you have been selected for the position of Senior Manual Instructor (Electrical Training Centre) at Newport Workshops.*
>
> *Signed S. F. Keane. C.M.E*

From second banana to Senior Instructor within a relatively short period was soon to bring in new talent. Kevin McPoyle followed from the plant shop with the retirement of Alf Robinson. His talents would come to the fore with input and initiatives. At year's end we took a breath to review the year and plan the replacement necessities, from tools to round steel and cast blocks for the next. The welcome for next year's intake was a mere couple of months away.

Metrification

Years after introduction of currency the steady progress towards measurement metrification continued. It gathered pace with the weight of the Australian Building Industry (AS 1155-1974) in July 1974 and like the rest of the industry our turn had come. Conversion charts of measurement were widely distributed and adaptions of the lathes progressively completed. To be followed by the shapers and milling machines as costs were allocated. Measuring instruments from micrometres to 6" rulers were in-hand. In the interim I had relationships to formalise and develop. Along with myself, other personnel in the apprentice system had changed. James Kain had taken the reins as the Principle at the VR College and Robert Baillee the Supervisor of Apprentices with the retirement of Roy Curtis in March of 1974. There were new kids on the block.

Independence or isolation?

In some ways the centre operated independently from the wider world. Other than the core of instructors, the centre had administration support by a junior clerk who managed the token board for attendance/absence and general admin tasks. The only regular face was the Supervisor of Apprentices usually linked to an individual apprentice's progress or personal family or accommodation needs. Bob Baillie; easy mannered and professional who had cut his teeth as a car builder supervisor. We were to work closely in progressing apprentices' needs.

Towards the middle of that following year, we had consolidated ourselves as the new team. The program and how the skills were imparted had changed little, if at all in the past decade. When I asked about feedback from the location destinations there was silence. How did we get feedback from our management group?

Assumption 1: I reported to the workshop manager as no other reporting line had been confirmed.

Assumption 2: the Apprentice Advisory Board were the key decision makers in matters relative to training.

I decided, with the perceived independence of the role, to visit locations and talk to a sample of user branch electrical supervisors. Their message was akin to more variation in their skills and to have high achievers released earlier without disruption to their academic year. Something to consider? Another consideration was feedback from the instructors at the Caulfield Signal & Communication training complex. As this was the destination of a large percentage of the electrical fitters it was important that there was some continuity from our start point. With the 19-day month cycle (38-hour week) long approved within the industry and referred to as an extra day off (EDO) the instructors preferred to take a half day a fortnight. This provided me with the flexibility of movement outside of business hours.

On the 11/11/1975, G G Kerr sacks Labour Government and Prime Minister Whitlam. Malcolm Frazer becomes caretaker Prime Minister. The representation of 24 unions and employees listened to Gough Whitlam speak and to 'Maintain the rage'. I was one of the elected ATOF Newport representatives attending that lunchtime meeting at the city square.

Outward

The next question was the other skill centres. Apprentices were being trained at other organisations, so what were they doing? If you don't ask you will never know. After an informal chat with Jim Kain (Principle of VR College) about looking outward I decided that introductions and visits should commence. He provided me with an introduction at RMIT and subsequently I was offered an industry position on their electrical trade syllabus committee. Over the following months invitations were accepted to visit the SEC Training Centre and the Army Trade School at Balcombe on the Mornington Peninsula. The exchange of information and their agreement for use of some of their models/drawings were enlightening and would fill some now perceived shortfalls in our training. In point of fact, our training was high in comparison but there were aspects to consider.

> Flat 9
> 396 Riversdale Road
> Camberwell 3124
> 18th August 1976.
>
> To whom it may concern.
>
> I have known Dennis Joseph Denman for a period of ten years whilst I was Principal of the Victorian Railways Technical College before retiring on 10th September 1975. He has always possessed outstanding energy and ability and proceeded to the position of Senior Instructor in the Electrical Division of Apprenticeship Training of the Victorian Railways.
>
> In his position he is doing an excellent job of work and knowing his proven ability I have no hesitation in recommending him for any position commensurate with his ability knowing that with his sincerity he would not let himself or his employer down at any stage.
>
> Yours faithfully
> James Blair
> Retired
> Principal VRT College

Letter of recommendation (1976)

The observable shortfall was the dependency/use on steel or cast iron. The characteristics and working/machining of other materials, non-ferrous (brass, aluminium and plastics) were missing. As a group, we agreed the benefits of some changes and these materials opened the door to the difference of tool and drill sharpening and machine cutting speeds. The next step was to introduce models and tools made from a composite of these materials, for example, a soft mallet using aluminium blanks at 2 inches (50 mm) diameter by 3 inches (75 mm) long. The end caps were plastic and brass, screw fitted at either end. The head was fitted with a cane handle by the car builder apprentices. One small model/tool had opened the door to both training centres and provided a learning experience to both groups. The support of Cliff Clarke (Car Builder Instructor) was invaluable. More than neighbours, we now had an overlap of common work.

Numero uno but still second banana

The constant in the daily tool or model making was the work bench, with six apprentices allocated to a bench. Each contained an individual tool locker and six positioned benchtop 4" jaw vices. On most days this was the work point were the grunt and bite of hand files and the patience of surface scrapping was your lot. This was also my second banana position in support of Doc Little. Doc was old school and if the outcome was to be flat, then it was non-negotiable. Though never discussed as a measurement the standard was .0001". One of the models was a surface plate that required using a blue marking paste on a master plate. The surface (model) on surface (master plate) blue rub indicated the high spots and this repeatable action and patient scrapping delivered a perfect flat surface. Undoubtably, I drove him to distraction as once more my skill level was challenged, and his exasperated, 'Mr Denman', had a familiar ring … time improved these skills.

The bloody block

Another task to which every generation of ETC apprentice would have common recall was the infernal chipping block. Every comment would undoubtably revolve around the frequency of attendance at the shops nurse with hand abrasions and worse. Why it had previously been overlooked as skill errors or collateral damage I'm unsure, but I viewed it differently. In my eyes a skill that should have been relegated to previous centuries was still on the books. The task involved chipping about a half inch (10 mm) from a 5 inch (100 mm) square cast iron block, an outdated skill where machine time and labour were today's main ingredients (in other words, the cost of labour to do the job).

The compromise was to use the 'shaper' machine to minimise the block's surface with the remainder to be hand chipped. The chipping skill maintained; the instances of hand abrasions declined. The continued sight of bandaids prompted the thought of first aid. Our industry had a long history of first aid practitioners and ambulance competitions. The first aid finals were a calendar highlight held annually at Mt Evelyn. Teams and individual competition were supported from statewide locations. Not only in-house but competitions were also held between other State railways.

Knock on doors

The Chief Ambulance Officer was only a phone call away. I sounded out his capacity and resources to train fifty odd apprentices yearly with the basic first year certificate. The next step was to make a case to the Apprentice Advisory Board on the benefits and application for the apprentice group. A program would be done in-house without loss to the skill program and provide a link to overall industry safety. The affirmative response set in motion their first aid training, examination and certification. Naturally each instructor joined the queue. My certificate was recorded in RS77/4345.

Another year on and the first thought of expansion was beginning to formalise. The training centre was boxed in on one side by the test laboratory but had ample room to take space from an under-utilised storage area adjacent. Negotiation commenced with Eric Mills, the Carriage Superintendent, for an area of approximately 20 square metres. Another affirmative, but with reservation. The sweetener: we had man (boy) power at our disposal and would supervise all manual handling and material relocation.

Together Kevin Mc and I redrew the new boundaries that would define the electrical section. Manual skills had a wide interpretation and should reflect the needs of today's industry and technology. I was clear eyed that some change was in need as the board circuits were the same as my first year at RMIT in 1961.

Half a house

Our vision was an uptake in electrical trade skills to include motor starter circuits to compliment the board work for light circuits. This led to our best decision of replicating a section of a house wall at lock up stage. Our objective was to supplement circuit board work with this framed section. A little initiative, access to timber for top and bottom plates and much more and skilled builders. The timber was requisitioned against our cost centre and the car builder apprentices had the opportunity of their life. Under supervision we built the half of a house frame, two parallel walls to building industry standard at about 4 metres with a window opening, and a half wall at the same length. A portion of each frame was covered with chip board and the majority open framed. All battened down and secured, it grew in the space of a week and was years ahead of its time in the application of the trade. It was to take more than two decades for me to observe this application in trade training at Trade & Further Education (TAFE). The translation of a simple single switch light, 2-way switching or mixed light and power circuits was an easy sell, their application visible and transferable because of the environment. Cables clipped cables fed, noggins drilled, light fittings and power points positioned and tested.

Other benefits with reorganising space enabled a vacated space to be modified for a lecture room. Instead of model drawing and blueprints being copied or discussed at lunch tables we could now provide a suitable room. The last positive was 'tool box' talks for machine/hand tool safety for small groups and study. On a roll, we looked outside the box, our next step was our connection to Richo and the plant shop.

We were looking to utilise any short cable lengths and offcuts that could be made available for the centre's use. Easy win and maybe we could help. Additionally, I had reviewed the store's inventory of items made by the plant shop for the workshops. Consumables like welding cables with fittings and extension leads with protective lamps were small job runs. Our offer was for the benefit of both parties. We would make the items on behalf of the plant shop if they provided the cable/fittings. The potential for variety was in place without disrupting the skill-based program.

The changes kept coming

Outside the compound other changes were occurring. Different roles required different skills so I had completed a short course of training and techniques with the Australian Organisation for Quality Control (night school again for 6 weeks) that confirmed my credentials and our instruction was current and relevant. Higher on the scale, our family was enriched with the birth of my son, but his impact caused hardly a ripple in Newport. A week's leave followed deriving the benefit of the recent maternity/paternity leave agreement. Like all new fathers, uninterrupted sleep took on a new pleasure.

For the later years, my rides to work had been divided between the Alamein to Camberwell shuttle and shop's train to Newport and my 145 Volvo. Our residence was strategically placed about five minutes from the Ashburton Station. I was a convert to train travel with almost door to door service. Sometime during this period, the Alamein shuttle came under threat with efficiencies implied by recommendations of the earlier Bland report. Among them, opening railways to competition from the road transport operators the rationalisation of freight operations and nearer home the closure of many of the less profitable lines. The local community was up in arms with any suggestion of the loss or changes to their rail transport. The save our trains committee was quickly launched with support by the local member for Burwood, the newly elected MLA Jeff Kennett. The outcome (regardless of the MLA's rhetoric) was never in doubt as the majority of this postcode had both economic and electoral clout.

Another day in another year and the benefits of our previous decisions were validated. The core skills programs continued with our enhancements. The progress of the second and third year apprentices was well integrated with their day release and college attendance. The college teachers were onside with our material changes. The crossover between theory and practice was beneficial for our learning outcomes. The previous year, the cadre of high-performance apprentices were able to be released to their locations or depots prior to the year's end. Accordingly, the centre now had a program and exit framework for the top 10%. Admittedly an informal arrangement between departments, but one of benefit to the higher skilled and quicker apprentices.

Drown or smother

My skill development progressed as second banana with acceptable improvement in my hand skills and measurements. Beyond my distractions, other highlights should be recorded. The induction of each new intake included a period of fire risk, fire appreciation and suppression. This activity was managed and operated by the local in-house firemen with a talk and practical demonstration, hoses and extinguishers.

In groups of about 12 to 15, apprentices were taken from our compound to the oval. Central to the shops was a large area of open space maintained and mowed for meal break recreation. Regardless of how they left they always arrived resembling drowned rats. The exercise included fire suppression of both material (wood scraps) and oil fires in a half 44-gallon drum. The finale was having two or three apprentices rolling out a 3" (75 mm) hose without pressure. Hit the tap and watch as they attempted to hold and direct a high-pressure hose. The results were spectacular and the firemen appreciable of their work. No apprentices were ever lost.

Next roll of the dice

A number of issues were bubbling along and led me to research and find some precedents of a work value case. The instructors from the boilermakers and carriage builders' trade centres were seeking some parody with the foremen's section and increased responsibility. The research was thorough, the comparison accurate and other factors highlighted to learning outcomes. The result summarised in the following:

Paint Manual Training Centre. Newport W/S

Dennis, may I on my behalf thank you for your foresight and endeavour in the action you took that we now enjoy the pay rise we received. Personally, to say that I am not more than pleased would be an understatement.

Regards, Cliff Clark.

Another year and the faces of many of the hundreds of young men began to fade except those top percent who were always in your face because of their talent and personality. Here Kevin Mc and I were at an advantage as we created the different and distractions. How Doc remembered them by name and progress was a marvel, but then he was the heart of the centre. Time and time again Neil Mac's reverie brought a smile. *All clerks are bastards, but not all bastards are clerks.* Such as this impersonal note from within the bowels of the granite house:

MC78/2436   Chief Mechanical Engineer's Office,
                                4th October, 1978

Memorandum: Manual training Instructor Mr. D.J. Denman applied for payment of sick leave and attached a note from Dental Surgeon Mr. G.A. Andrews for dental treatment <u>in the morning</u>. It is reasonable to assume that an officer may be incapacitated for a

ELECTRICAL TRAINING CENTRE – A NEW CALLING

> *full shift if extractions are involved, but where fillings etc. only are concerned there is no valid reason why resumption of duty cannot be undertaken. It is proposed to approve payment in this instance but…please so inform him.*

Metrification continued

Our next step was to review our metrification program in respect to our machine/turning work, small fry in the big picture, but part of our progression. Following the conversion of our monitory system, metrification was proceeding by timetable. Every industry or manufacturer or food suppliers had target dates for completion. For example, dairy products, 1972–1974, oil industry and petrol pumps by 1974-1976, and locomotives and rolling stock at 75% by 1978.

In point of fact, the conversion adaptors for the lathes were adequate but our review suggested higher standards. Notwithstanding that training lathe operatives was not our primary objectives, the machining of tool and model sections required exacting measurements. Top of our review was to validate a case for new lathes. The market place provided the options of make and models and the value case written up for the Apprentice Advisory Committee to consider. Someone in high office, the CME's office (L.C Rolls acting CME) supported the case, and within a short time the Production Engineers' Department provided a layout and changeover program. At days end, with the new infrastructure of 10 new lathes locked and wired, the Electrical Training Centre was in our eyes the leader in apprentice electrical trade skills.

Our position may have been confirmed with an unannounced visit by a group including Graeme Swift, Workshop Manager, Bob Baillee, (Supervisor of Apprentices) and Bill Hunter, Education Officer (Corporate Personnel). Of course, this was conjecture. Outside of the work hours, self-development and learning were part of my DNA. I had continued with a night course and completed a cinematograph operator's licence course (Licence No. 3860). Films on safety could be hired free from the government film centre and this occasionally added a change to the apprentices learning days.

The clock was ticking and a casual reference to a vacancy in the Weekly Notice was drawn to my attention. Reflecting the times, job vacancies were also advertised in open competition in the *Saturday Age*. The lure was increased salary and specifically, an opportunity for advancement for those who show initiative, creativeness and are effective in their position.

> *Training officers (2 positions) created to meet the specialised training needs of our personnel in the Melbourne Underground Rail Loop (MURL). Applications setting out details of experience and qualifications through respective Heads of Branch with appropriate recommendations to reach the Director of Personnel, Room 102, Head Office by 8th June 1979.*

The process of interview and presentation occurred raising an element of hope.

LM: JAC   Chief Mechanical Engineer's Office
                 22 June, 1979 Memorandum:
Senior Manual Instructor. Mr D J Denman is the successful applicant for the recently advertised position of Training Officer

---

ELECTRICAL TRAINING CENTRE – A NEW CALLING

> *with the Personnel Branch. He is to be instructed to transfer to head office and report to Room 102, on Monday 25.6.79. Acting Chief Mechanical Engineer.*

Three days after receiving this memo, my time at the Electrical Training Centre at Newport ended. Who knows if we enhanced the progress of that period of apprentices. I like to think for the majority, yes.

The years following saw both Graham Button and then Graeme Copeland at the centre's helm. The pathway from the plant shop was clearly established and far from my eyeline. Changes continued in the following years as the ETC was relocated from the East Block nearer the technical college.

Regrettably I was to not to play a role in future apprentice training or witness the demise of the skill centres.

CHAPTER 10

CORPORATE TRAINING AND MURLA – SUITS AND TIES

Once more my papers were stamped and my time at Newport Workshops belonged to another decade. After a period of stability and promotion within the trade, the future was linked to a major capital works endeavour, the Melbourne Underground Rail Loop. Change had occurred at a frightening rate with three days' notice to 'pack my bags'. A quiet thankyou to the team and the hope that the program would remain beneficial, then it was goodbye. It was also a break in many ways from a social structure, the organisation and branch that had employed me from January 1961.

The VR Board had replaced the Victorian Railways Commissioners and we now traded as VicRail. The new functional organisation was in place and my past now consumed under the Assistant General Manager Technical. Although separated by a mere 13 kilometres, the distance between the CBD and Newport might have been a hundred kilometres as the impact of organisational change seeped to the level of the workforce. I not only changed location into the heady heights of personnel, but also into a different mindset. It was a new world where the dirt and grime of physical work was left far behind. Where previously everyone was clearly labelled by a boiler suit or a dust coat, suits and ties differentiated the workforce and the overhead. In some ways this promotion by location and salary was also a step backwards. My years of being a practising supervisor/manager of people and resources were set aside and ignored as I set about this new role or responsibility. This was a different environment where I was to start again.

Once more Flinders Street Station became my destination and this time as a resident in the upper floors and not looking up from the platforms. A tie and suit were a little different from my previous garb with a step ladder and fluorescent tubes at hand. Much had happened in the past decade in both transport and my role. Yet nothing new in a changed location. Fortunately, I was not solo, as it was the case of not one but two. The other successful candidate was possibly equally apprehensive but there he was in his brown suit and tie, equally looking forward to this new challenge.

Ray Page and I were to form the nucleus of the Melbourne Underground training. Ray's background was as a signaller and had heightened his profile by completing the RMIT transport certificate. We sort of arrived at the Flinders Street Station building after the introductions to Hilton Ludikins at head office. The Training and Development section sat high above the bustle of the suburban platforms in rooms that were part of the fourth floor annex. It was a building in neglect and although the home of the education section and many functions of the VRI, on the second floor its iconic status was far removed from previous architectural highlights. From here Bill (William) Hunter managed and coordinated the corporate programs with oversight by an advisory council of Assisting General Managers. The arrival of Ray and I was around the same time as other appointments in the fields of training research and customer relations. Change was well past the byword of the day; it was an ever constant. Our immediate priorities were our new work environment and peers and fast tracking our knowledge about the underground (MURLA).

Starting with the training section (T&D), its objective might be surmised to establish aspects of leadership programs that were not presently provided by the past organisational structure. New initiatives were being introduced in support of the organisation, including a Supervisors' Productivity Achievement Program. Other ongoing examples were the supervisor's courses and a separate middle management training course instituted in 1973. The section additionally provided a Train the Trainer course based on the Department of Labour & Immigration TOP (Training Officers Program). Equally high on their achievements was the Kids in Danger program and English classes. The Kids in Danger program had been developed as a joint initiative between the VR Education Section and the Victorian Police. The program promoted child safety awareness and was taken to schools and also presented to minor infringement breakers.

Peers and others

The assembly of peers was to identify some faces previously known to me and many of different backgrounds. Our manager, Bill Hunter was a tall athletic figure, cultured and widely read. He was friendly and quickly set up the options for the different work groups who would be working in or associated with the underground environments. Frank Hall was nominally 2IC with a background in safety. The *VR Newsletter* of October 1964 reports Mr C F Hall as the VR Safety Guidance Officer. Frank was old school, pedantic and lacked warmth. Others included Ron Jenkins, ex-Rolling Stock safety officer and now leading the supervisors and middle management programs. Ron welcomed us with genuine pleasure and as another example of promotion from within the grades. He and I had links to the workshops and if one was needed, a suitable role model.

Alan Whitla was involved in trainer training programs, general research and ingratiating self-promotion. He in previous years had been part of the guards' training committee whose charter was to improve existing safe working standards and investigate a more productive examination method for guard trainees. Their recommendations supported by the general studies division of RMIT was successfully piloted but ultimately not accepted. Oral questioning continued as the preferred examination format. Key committee members included Peter Helbig, (Manager Stations Operations) Bill Oehm (ARU) and Bill Hunter (Education Officer). The committee's final report is now held at the PMI's Victorian Railway collection. This surely was an example of the resistance to modern testing options by the ARU and the impotency of a management group.

Alan, who was to become a future confident, had found his way from the Accountancy Branch. Alan was located at the Princes

Gate Staff Training Centre, the former Princes Gate Restaurant beneath the plaza at Princes Gate. This dedicated centre was a resource of opportunity and was used by others for seminars and major presentations. Regular first aid courses and welfare presentations were in-train. Notably seminars on topics, including problem drinkers within the industry. The *VR Newsletter* records, 'VicRail drinkers are off the rails, presented by welfare officers, Dick Mills and Wes Gordon'.

Would anyone be interested in the final 12 months of my apprenticeship at that very location? I doubted it then, even more now. Even towers can be felled with political will. Indeed, in future years these twin towers named for the Gas & Fuel occupants did fall under a different political regime. Still others played significant roles but they were for another time.

Upskill the new boys

Within a short period of our arrival at T&D, Ray Page and I were in self-development mode as part of the 'TOP program, Stage 1, Group Instructional Techniques undertaken by the Department of Training & Immigration'. This training officer program provided a pathway for all its attendees to build through its three stages. Stage 1 opened the door that enabled each facet of a training process to be broken down and then presented to a group forum. The syllabus included setting objectives, session planning, communication skills, how people acquire knowledge and a systems approach to training. Each trainee completed a number of 10-minute skill and knowledge or informational sessions. The diversity of the group brought many a different skill to each session. The trainers at Windsor created a learning environment that supported both the learner, the process and their presentation. The program brought us together with other trainers from the wider industry and commercial world and enabled us to gauge our skill set against wider competition. Both on track and in the higher percentile. A fortnight later we left with an increased degree of confidence.

TOP program participants, 1980, author left, centre row

Melbourne Underground Rail Loop Authority, MURLA

The Authority that had overall management and control had been literally digging under the streets of Melbourne for years. Test bores had been undertaken by the Mines Department from as early as 1961. Once more a fleeting connection as during my time at the Princes Gate Section we had undertaken fault repairs on the test pump near Wellington Parade.

CORPORATE TRAINING AND MURLA – SUITS AND TIES

Tunnelling works under the city had commenced in June 1972. The construction of the tunnels coincided with the new elevated viaduct section between Flinders Street and Spencer Street, the three new underground stations (Parliament, Museum and Flagstaff) and the Metrol train control complex. On completion, the underground or 'Loop' was to be fully integrated with the suburban train system. Four separate tunnels each with an average length of 3.74 kilometres were constructed using a tunnel boring machine, cut and cover and other mining methods.

Our start point was access to all the information and specifications that could readily be adapted for training purposes. Bill Hunter arranged for us to meet with the VR Underground Loop Project Liaison Officer, Mr E Rudolph. Ernie's previous position was as the Deputy Chief of the Electrical Engineering Branch and he'd taken over the role following the elevation of Mr R Gallacher to the Director of Planning. Ernie was interested in our role and interesting in his role. Initially, he was the doorway to the various parties of the authority, enabling access to their treasure including photographs, plans and diagrams, and he became a secondary boss, with regular meetings and progress reports.

Our other main source of shape and form came with our introduction to the team of the Graphic Arts Department managed by Michael Ball. Within this group resided a skill base that complimented every suggestion in either print form or visual imaging. Both Ray and I were to rely heavily on their refinement of our promotions and ideas These many years later, the support of the manager's secretary who was the sole source of typing our draft notes and presentations was exemplary. Well done, Marie. It was a time prior to individual personal computers and their introduction in future years would silence the chatter of the Olivetti typewriters.

MURL management presentation, L–R: D Denman,
R Page, W Hunter (Manager T&D),
E Rudolf, (MURL coordinator)

From our room on the fourth floor, we were daily on the move between the locations as we refined the mediums that were to be our base teaching/training resources. As we were both new to the idea of mass population information/training we were guided into processes that had currency and use of available technology. The guidelines were shaped to develop a number of self-paced booklets that could be used independently or as a resource for instructional sessions. Additionally, we would follow a recent successful audio/visual slide program utilised for dangerous goods. These tape/slide presentations were not quite a CinemaScope epic but could be developed by a scripted voice over to a matching slide to a give a small cinematic experience. They were cost-effective and we had an experienced resource at hand. The photographic section and Kevin Baker, a sort of T&D enigma who wrote and produced the in-house magazine *Personnelities* was on hand with his contacts. During this collection and research period, we additionally had access to the draft information that was intended for public consumption for MURLA publicity. In some ways we were ahead of their curve.

Sydney-bound

Dialogue between Bill Hunter and his NSW Rail equivalent had led to the offer of a visit to observe the Sydney Eastern Suburban Rail section. This rail extension of new underground stations at Redfern, Central, King's Cross, Edgecliff and Bondi Junction, provided new services to the eastern suburbs and its densely populated community. Opened in June of 1979 it incorporated many services that were to be used in the MURL. The opportunity to talk to our counterparts and share ideas was warmly received and soon two MURL training officers were Sydney-bound.

Departing on the evening *Southern Aurora* we arrived and were met in Central for a shared show and tell and information exchange. Although we partnered in most aspects of the proposed programs each of us had brought different knowledge and skill sets. Ray's background in operational running and signalling immediately implied that Metrol, the new central control centre would be his best match while I concentrated on the general information programs. Representatives of NSW Rail were both informative and sharing in their materials and products, and during a site visit to an underground station we observed their system operation and the public infrastructure in a working environment. All the new stations were provided with an automatic ticket fare collection system with ticket vending machines and automatic barriers. This experience was invaluable and our thanks lost in our only problem … an interstate train strike that left us scrambling for help. The T&D office came good with return home flights and two overwrought travellers returned late that night to Victorian soil.

Workforce training

Soon, with finished products, we were undertaking informational and training programs to managers and selected operational staff. Staff at each key integrating stations, Richmond, Spencer Street and Flinders Street were the priority with all other station grades gradually introduced to support customer enquiries. One by memory was a personal disaster as a first-time presenter to the Corporate Heads. The program itself was fine, but my nerves were on show. My confidence grew with every session.

During this period, I was tasked to present an informational session to a combined group of the Victorian police and fire officers at the Metropolitan Fire Brigade (MFB) Abbotsford Training Centre. Complimentary pass, so we moved on. The training packages for Metrol had been distributed and Ray was progressively meeting key signalling personnel. Metrol was a purpose-built train control complex fronting Batman Avenue and adjacent to the Power Operations Centre now labelled as Electrol. The original function of Metrol was to be the main train control centre facility for the Melbourne suburban railways, as well as to be the signal box for the City Loop. The spread of information beyond the rail operators to the State's essential services was growing incrementally, as the first phase of the loop opening approached. With the assistance of Kevin Baker, two separate tape/slide programs, Metrol and MURL had been completed with multiple copies. Titled 'City

CORPORATE TRAINING AND MURLA – SUITS AND TIES

Loop an overview' and 'Metrol the Central Control Centre', these self-managed informational sessions with their accompanied question and answer booklets were distributed system-wide for local training.

Much had been accomplished in the period dedicated to the training and assimilation of operating and station staff within the underground environment. Both Ray and I had donned hard hats, safety vests and walked suburban drivers and guards through the completed tunnels as well as essential service personnel as required. We had digested every part of the Museum Station from its lowest level to its main foyer and mezzanine levels. The number of station levels, the length and depth of the elevators and the location of every service and system … we held the library of systems and services linked to the loop and the proposed operational sequences and control points. We became go-to men and had walked the tunnels from Museum, now Central station to the Spencer Street portals. At our fingertips we had the trivia of tunnel sizes, below the street levels depth and every service in both the system and station. Others were working in concert with the construction authority as more and more services were tested and came on line. Alan Dockery was managing the Museum Station's facilities programs and the Australian Federated Union of Locomotive Enginemen (AFULE) was prominent in their prerequisites for driver training. We never claimed the 'underground allowance'.

Many other groups were coming together before the opening of the plaza atop the Museum Station by Queen Elizabeth II in May 1980. Traction power was turned on in October 1980 and the first train ran on December 1980. To the best of my memory our invites went astray. We had not been involved in the grime or environment of the tunnelling process, yet without ever lifting a pick understood the impact the Loop would have on our industry and wider community. A significant event to be part of. The Loop was progressively opened with the Burnley and Caufield tunnel services in January 1981, followed by the Clifton Hill/City Circle Group and Parliament Station and finally in 1985, the Northern loop and the Flagstaff Station.

CHAPTER 11

BEYOND MURL – CUSTOMER RELATIONS

This period had been fulfilling and enabled me to be see first-hand the world of train operations. On reflection after attending the Stage 1 Training Officers Program (TOP) we recognised that the bar had been lifted to remain competitive. Our application for a salary increment had been rejected, citing criteria that was plainly incorrect. Another example of ... *all clerks are bastards, but not all bastards are clerks.* The memo, dated 5/3/1981, noted that:

> '... *salary increments for Messrs: R Page and D Denman will be considered after the respective anniversary dates of their appointment.*'

We were appointed 25 June 1979? Appeal or roll with the punches.

The influx of external staff was either teacher trained or graduates. These observations were consolidated in my private space. At monthly evening meetings of the Institute of Management (I had been a member for a number of years) their research indicated the take up of retiring AIF service members (who could retire at age 50) and teachers due to uncompetitive pay rates. It could be surmised that initiative and a history of results had lessened for insiders in the T&D section.

Our response (independently) was Ray's acceptance at RMIT for a Diploma in Organisational Behaviour, while I signed on for an Associate Diploma of Education. Years later Bill Hunter's words would hit home, 'suggesting time spent in self-education might as well be a degree/diploma instead of a lesser qualification'.

An integral part of the TOP program was a contract to complete an in-house assignment. My referral was to the Electrical Engineering Branch with past memories of the Light & Power section and my High Voltage Switching certification. My appointment was with Bill Wilkins the Chief Engineer where he clarified his needs. Bill was an erudite and warm individual who quickly confirmed a needs analysis against the present program for training linesmen. The linesmen's school was at the time located at Port Melbourne and had a dedicated instructor. Training was a mixture of operational procedure and material handling to complement their 'trade' skills. With access to the work group and location, a detailed report and recommendations were provided to the CEE.

Any concerns about being relegated or pigeonholed to aspects of trade training were quickly put to bed as other needs arose. Paralleling the MURL program and our appointments was the introduction of a customer relations program for station and freight centre staff. Other dedicated staff and a research officer was employed to promulgate this 'to be developed course'. The son of a highly regarded leading hand in the EE Branch was an appointment, Theo Spanos. Wet behind the ears, personable and ambitious, he and others from the retail world would stay only a brief time.

Something new, customer relations

This CR course was undertaken at our training rooms located on the third floor. With a number of rooms dedicated on this level, the priority MURL and Customer Relations training worked hand in hand. Foremost initially was station staff for the Customer Relations course which was a positive management initiative. Each course was opened and endorsed by the branch head. Jack Draper was a visible identity within his responsibilities as Chief Transport Manager. His presence warmly acknowledged by his workforce and added clout to the trainers.

Regrettably, many station staff were a little nonplussed by suits extolling the principles of customer interactions when they had been 'at the coal face' for periods of years. A somewhat difficult scenario to rationalise for the bulk of our CR presenters with little or no direct experience in rail operations to my knowledge. Had they ever been visible to the public at a ticket barrier as the peak bustled pass? Or abused because of train delays or cancellations out of their control? Even as we became advocates of the CR program, maybe we too missed the point. My out was several years as a market researcher in many face-to-face exchanges.

Soon the team of Page and Denman were reassembled to continue the CR course. In many ways we were spoiled and provided coffee and biscuits as part of every course. This was a normal part of most professional training and enabled a start point and informal welcome and introduction. Who would have considered the feedback from some station staff that indicated that 'in the many years' they had never been offered a coffee from management. Many who worked permanent morning and late shifts saw little of their supervisors so even this experience was strangely uplifting.

Customer relations to the bush

The regional centres were now added to our training population, including freight centre and operational and station staff. The locations rolled by as the Page & Denman team became a travelling show. With the mandate of management and good work by local roster staff the 'show' reached further faces with increased participation. The *Sunraysia* edition of the day headlined the following:

> 'Training talks for VicRail.' The first of a number of customer relations training program for country VicRail staff was held in Mildura yesterday ... It is hoped that eventually more than 8000 VicRail staff from country areas will have participated. Customer relations training has been operating in Melbourne for the past 12 months and during this time 1000 members have taken part.

We completed a busy schedule before I returned to Windsor for Stage 2 of the TOP program. The syllabus included identifying training as an overall process that incorporated an analysis of the work environment, the worker (position description), the work required and the method of undertaking the work. The consolidation of this process combined organisational case studies and a visit to a host company that provided a work role for

BEYOND MURL – CUSTOMER RELATIONS

Bendigo, Customer Relations session publicity, 1982

Mildura *Sunraysia* article, 1982.

review and analysis. The trainers at Windsor created a learning environment that supported both the learner, the process and their presentation. It became the blueprint for all future training needs analysis and required a 4-week in-house assignment to be completed. I completed an analysis of the driver training program by activity and timelines.

Unsure whether or not I had reached my peak, some observations were being confirmed as the numbers and competition continued to grow. The teaching profession had arrived. Vacancies at wider locations were soon on my list. Competitiveness seemed to be a palpable commodity within this group far in excess of my previous environments. My contact with Newport was not entirely severed, I had returned for brief outings for retirement functions including Alf Pugh's retirement. During this period the turnstile at the manager's office had revolved with names like Swift and Carney passing through. With changes to the plant shop personnel, I had become an outsider dressed in a tie and suit and associated with head office.

Aspects of apprentice training had also changed, with the completion of the first stage of the Newport Technical College. The college reputedly on a 99-year lease was situated fronting Champion Road on acres within the western boundary of the Newport workshops. A new vision of training was now in place as our apprentices joined private and other community wide apprentices. The Victorian Railway College ceased in 1980.

The position of Supervisor of Apprentices had become vacant. I was drawn to the role but somewhat dubious about a return to the Newport location. Toss of the coin but my hat went into the ring. I was unsuccessful.

BEYOND MURL – CUSTOMER RELATIONS

> *Memo: GS:SE:220. To Training Inst. Mr D. Denman, per Director of Personnel. I regret to inform you that your application for the position of Supervisor of Apprentices at Newport via weekly notice no 31 & 32/80 was unsuccessful. Foreman N.A. Morison of Newport Workshops has been selected for the position. If you wish to appeal………Chief Manager, Workshops. 10th November 1980*

So be it. However, the interview experience was one that remained a long memory, not for the result but the process. The three-person panel consisting of representatives from personnel, management and independent was a standard format, but … my presentation supporting my experience in the area of specific responsibilities and my qualifications, past and current might have been relevant. From one individual, let's call him Frank, questions along the lines of, 'You have a reputation of being single-minded and difficult', followed by, 'Would you be able to dismiss or relocate instructors that you had previously worked with?' My silence said it all …

That a panel member would even contemplate the aforementioned was an indictment on the process and said little about his objectivity. An appeal was never on; and my interest lost forever. Such a pity that I didn't have the foresight to include my reference from the retired Principle of the VR Technical College. Or to tell them to stick it.

> To whom it may concern. I have known Dennis Joseph Denman for a period of 10 years whilst I was Principle of the Victorian Railway Technical College before retiring. He has always possessed outstanding energy and ability

> and proceeded to the position of Senior Instructor. I have no hesitation in recommending him for any position commensurate with his ability knowing that with his sincerity he would not let himself or his employer down at any stage. Yours faithfully, James R Kain.

At Spring Street there was major change. Rupert Hamer resigned in June of 1981 enabling his deputy Lindsay Thompson to become Premier. Local media suggested Melbourne had benefited from the Hamer government years by inciteful legislation and modernisations including, the arts and transport. With Thompson's elevation, Robert MacLennan became the new Minister of Transport. Hamer had succeeded by taking a brush to the privation period of the Bolte Government.

The first of the Comeng trains were now on line with new livery and air-conditioning, a selling point for customers. Courses continued on the FSS third floor with hardly a ripple. Change was also apparent at T&D. The wheels of employment continued to turn and the section was beginning to resemble a school of advanced education. T&D was looking better by the day.

A win and some losses

I had won the position of Senior Training Officer in the section. I was unsuccessful for the position of Principle Training Officer, (Divisional Training & Consultancy Services). Tertiary qualifications were key criteria. With resignations and retirements, other faces soon appeared. Ex-teacher Paul Woodbridge was employed for the English classes. Rod Wilke, ex-army, was employed as a Senior

BEYOND MURL – CUSTOMER RELATIONS

Training Officer, shortly followed by Don Matthews and Paul Hanrahan. Nicholas Constantino was another insider to join our ranks. Nick was a fresh-faced individual with a high work ethic who shared with me a daily shuttle commute between Alamein and Camberwell to FSS as Ashburton was our home station.

Jostling for position soon became apparent, as the face of our management changed. Rumours of disharmony was hushed as the female teacher of the Kids program resigned. John Lunn was imported from the commercial world and Bill Hunter off to Personnel. The ruffling of feathers within Bill Hunter's cadre was short lived as they sought other mentors. Somewhere within this period a murmur of them and us was beginning to surface. The Weekly Notice took on greater significance beyond its operational information ... it became the source of vacancies or opportunities.

Although little more than a backdrop to working in the industry, I still paid my dues to the Australian Transport Officers Federation. The function of the union had faded beyond Newport as the needs of work valuation and conditions seemed outside this remit. My interest had been piqued by the position of Chairman of the Classification Committee, Position B. I had a background in foreman classifications and work value experience, but it was pointed out that the probability was low given my lack of experience in other classifications and awards. A personnel branch appointment was confirmed. Memo ref: JD: IK:103.

My next distraction was a vacancy in the Office of Officers' and Employees' Representative on the Board of Discipline, and two deputies. These deputy positions would be the result of an independent voting system of officers and employees similar to a council vote. My eligibility was confirmed for a deputy on the Board, 12 nominations confirmed my name on the voting roll.

Once again, I came up short. The support of the operations grade unions, ARU in a nominee was a difficult task for an independent candidate.

Candidate	Rank, grade in railway service	Votes polled
Denman, Dennis Joseph	Senior Training Officer	3347
Gillespie, David George	Rel Station Master	3179
Hibbert, Arthur William	Suburban Guard	4114
Thompson, James	Arthur Station Officer	4446

Management shake-up

Whether conjecture or not, middle management was seen to require access to wider business techniques and systems. Built on previous decisions, two programs were selected by the executive group to be run in-house: The Chandler and Macleod's personality types and the Kepner Tregoe Problem Solving/Decision Making workshops. KT is a problem analysis model in which the problem is disconnected from the decision, via analysing potential risks and opportunities. It was a period of high expectations for individuals with the skill set to present these programs in-house and I was to join the team to be accredited as a trainer. I had to earn my spurs.

Outside our programs, a selection of senior managers commenced at the Mount Eliza Business Course. The business of the VicRail management was moving ever forward. I was soon to complete the week's Chandler & Macleod trainer course presented at Kew and join the supervisor/management team. I joined Ron Jenkins as a senior presenter. This course delivery or presentation became my staple role with a steady stream of supervisors finding their way to the training rooms on the third floor. In a matter of months few conversations could be had in-house without the inferred reference to a personality type and how they might be approached or disciplined. Not dissimilar to the Myers-Briggs selection process the Chandler & MacLeod program addressed the Behaviour B=f (P.E) equation and then the individual temperaments and combinations and how to best manage individual types.

It was impressed on all attendees that it was a study of an individual over time (observation) to realise the best results. The other positive of the course was some insight into the individual's personality, strengths and weaknesses and an understanding that temperament is not a barrier to performance. Hopefully the training was to be used in context of the introduction of annual reviews.

Historically, pay increments for salary grades were almost an automatic progression with a tick to performance. Modern systems and techniques were to enable a two-way conversation between the parties to identify performance and areas of improvement. This course was to provide the reference points and techniques for these reviews. Unforeseen at the time was the use in the future of staff reviews within the T&D section that was to cause angst and union intervention. A sabbatical was in store.

The new manager confirmed I was to attend the Stage 3 of the Training Officer Program as part of my continued self-development. With little regret for the ongoing courses, I happily progressed to this next level of training. The break from the changes was welcomed. I watched as the needy circled and positioned themselves for the new regime. Surprisingly (or not) my lifestyle and social circle continued mostly away from my work group, yet day by day shared experiences or course responsibilities impacted the group dynamics. Notwithstanding, I would continue to value the time spent in business hours, but hadn't formed any particular dependent relationships. Whether a defensive mechanism by me or not we were competitors for future positions. It was quickly established that the difference between John Lunn and Bill Hunter was chalk and cheese. Where the former manager exuded energy and bounce, his replacement was pleasant but introspective and dour. This was to test the future group dynamics and other vacancies within the group.

CHAPTER 12

PRINCES GATE STAFF TRAINING CENTRE – THE BUNKER

Another ghost of the past as aspects of Princes Gate became my next work station. My role was to present the in-house Train the Trainer program as more of the divisions sought to qualify their technical and operational instructors in training techniques. Historically rail industry training was an engrained in-house branch responsibility and operated as a line management responsibility. Trainers were required from dedicated work grades including, shunter, refreshment staff, ganger, work protection, linesmen, undergear repairer, as well as station grades including station masters and signalman. The required training including safe working systems, first aid, safety, the list went on and on.

Exclusive to this list was driver training (suburban trains and locomotives) and apprentice training. The exception was the safe working classes previously coordinated and run by the Victoria Railway Institute, including correspondence papers for country and shift workers.

Linked to all these work units was countless roles of examiners and certifiers. My stay below ground might be for ever. I was to share the bunker and the presentation of early courses with Alan Whitla before an exclusive takeover. My review of the in-house course notes suggested that subtle changes that were current in the TOP program would benefit our instructors. My discussion with Alan arrived at; do as you think. He had other distractions, including a child on the way and was soon to be a participant to attend and review the Mt Eliza management program.

Wheels within wheels?

The refurbished bunker was a spacious open seminar/training area with an adjoining office, storerooms and large kitchen. Perfect for programs and the odd seminar but a location/venue that should have been utilised for purpose, not as a daily work station. Separated by the width of Swanston Street it operated independently and in isolation. Visitors outside of course presenters were few, but as the bunker was also used for seminars, staff meetings and course reviews, total isolation was avoided. It was the location for the section's staff meeting including organisational updates by both subsequent Personnel/HR managers, Hilton Ludikins and Peter Stuart followed by Denis Watts. Sunlight and weather of any type was forgotten under the glare of fluorescent lights. It became an imperative to seek the green of the river bank and surrounds in most lunch breaks.

PRINCES GATE STAFF TRAINING CENTRE – THE BUNKER

Alan and I combined well and concluded the shared courses with a tribute to the English comedians, Ronnie Barker and Ronnie Corbet, it's 'good bye from me and good bye from him'. Finally, an aspect of humour, repeating the motto, that training should be fun. The numbers grew as the pool of instructors completed the course. Some by personality would be better than other but all met the criteria of instructional techniques and presentation. Each participant's skill/information session was videoed and the tapes reviewed by peer and presenter feedback. Additionally, this medium was available for self-critique and any assistance I could provide. It was a collegiate period and satisfying time with the realisation that you have been instrumental in another's development.

The conclusion of each course was celebrated in style. Someone had contacts in the refreshment branch and we accepted the spread of mixed sandwiches and the odd dozen brown bottles. For those that kicked on after 1730 lock-up, Young & Jacksons was near at hand. The bunker remained my work space for a year or so as our numbers waxed and waned. Tony Yacono had arrived form Myers as part of the customer relations team. Tony was a gifted presenter and helped in improved aspects of communication styles in our in-house course. Others had resigned or taken roles in other divisions.

Rail collision

Months before the change of government the Barnawartha site was the place of collision between the *Spirit of Progress* and a goods train. The collision which occurred in heavy fog became the second major disaster on the Sydney–Melbourne route following the *Southern Aurora* many years previous. This incident added another distraction to the fourth floor workforce with colleagues in train running.

Months later and events of the state election hit the headlines. The Cain Labour party had won the 1982 election and Steve Crabb took the reins as the new Transport Minister. It was the forerunner of the splinter of the Training & Development training section as within the year, two new organisations determined their business structures. In 1983, VicRail was divided into the State Transport Authority, with responsibility for the provision of country rail and road passenger and freight services. The STA was to trade under the name of V/line. The Metropolitan Transit Authority was dedicated to the provision and responsibility over the suburban passenger operations. At staff meetings we had been briefed on these changes without any particular implications to the positions within the T&D section.

In March of 1983, Robert (Bob) Hawke led a new labour government to victory. It was the beginning of a significant number of national reforms that shaped today's Australia, including economic, award restructuring and the prices and incomes accord.

My next task was the Kepner Tregoe program. Once more the Melbourne to Sydney train took us northward into NSW, for my second visit after MURL. I accompanied Don Matthews on the second trainer course. Set in a venue in the Blue Mountains, we were to join a group of commercial managers and others of like ilk to be accredited for the program. It was a week of full learning and presentation and feedback. Feedback from our peer trainers and the KT team. This workshop followed the theme of group bonding and support to enhance the learning experience. As a fully integrated in-house experience the course was run for success. The sessions were spread between day and evening with social activities including mini tourist activities. Each participant had been issued with a trainer and a participant manual. Many hours of evening study linking the course notes (participant manual) guided by the trainer manual became the norm to meet our objectives as a credentialed presenter.

PRINCES GATE STAFF TRAINING CENTRE – THE BUNKER

I was to learn that the KT program is a structured methodology for gathering information and prioritising and evaluating it. It is a rational model well respected in business management circles. It may include any aspect of non-performance or potential opportunities for a business. We learned the four basic steps of situational appraisal, problem analysis, decision analysis and potential problem analysis. It is a critical decision analysis and the program provided case studies to action via our courses. This program was an eye-opener in confirming that the wider world of business was near at hand. Our peer group included representatives from businesses including the Bank of NSW, Qantas and Lysaght Steel. Pty Ltd.

Personal & Confidential

July 25, 1984

Mr Dennis Denman, Senior Training Officer, V/Line.
223 Flinders Street, Melbourne 3000.

Dear Dennis, congratulations on completing your first Problem Solving/Decision Making workshop. I was particularly impressed by your understanding of each of the processes; your teaching of each was very thorough … I have pleasure in giving you your certificate. This licenses you to run KT workshops at V/Line in accordance with the terms of our agreement.

Yours sincerely, Kepner-Tregoe A'asia Pty Ltd,
M.J. Keaney, Associate.

Another program, this time in partnership with Ron Jenkins and Don Matthews, as the weekly course began an endless cycle. Ron and I became the senior presenters with Don moving to workshops. Once more I settled in to a period of course following course yet still managed some variation within the theme without loss of the program objectives or outcomes. Like the Chandler MacLeod course the organisation was coming to terms with a common vocabulary, including an analysis framework outside of rail operations.

These new authorities soon dictated the demise of the central T&D section as we began to assess our futures or options with either the STA or MTA. As these organisations solidified their needs, the business of course presentations continued.

The performance review fiasco

How it become a fiasco is unsure but one of our trainers who had been seconded to the section was tipped of about our reviews. Les Miles' background was within the clerical grades and he was a ATOF representative from his last position. He reputedly complained to the ATOF and they formally informed the personnel manager of a process undertaken outside agreed guidelines. The angst was that the T&D Manager had completed performance reviews without any discussion with individuals or provision for them to comment. The management/federation agreement for any performance reviews was an outcome between the manager and person being reviewed. No big deal was the response. A suggestion that the section was full of prima donnas was attributed to 67 Spencer Street but never confirmed. At a lunchtime meeting, it was requested that these reviews be withdrawn and destroyed without prejudice as the parties came together for a solution.

Meanwhile my original MURL partner Ray Page had applied and relocated to a vacancy in the State Government services for special duties in various departments. He was in future years to attain CEO status beyond transport. Regrettably this timing occurred with the failure of my marriage. I took extended leave to establish the next phase of my personal life. John Lunn and Alan Whitla were highly supportive during this period. As the 'storm in the teacup' found a solution, this period of discontent and accusations spread between the personnel manager and the majority of the training group. Other factors surely were in play as John Lunn resigned, followed by Tony Yacono. Tony was on his way to personal success, managing his own human resources business. Frank Hall inherited the section as the two authorities manned up. Rod Wilke moved to the MTA with a vision of a training empire. Shortly after, Frank, Alan and Theo headed into the personnel cloud of the STA training. Others made individual decisions and relocated. With no offers at hand my options became vacant positions or …

CHAPTER 13

STATE TRANSPORT AUTHORITY – 67 SPENCER STREET

The STA business model saw its organisational structure divided into two major head office groups and six regional groups. Accordingly, this structure was recorded in the *STA News* in September 1984. The Chief General Manager, Transport Operations explained, under the former VicRail organisation with its seventeen separate branches with a head reporting to four assistant general managers who in turn reported to a general manager, the process of decision-making tended to be somewhat slow and cumbersome. The new structure had clear lines of responsibility and authority with regions to be controlled by a manager and comprise, Central (Melbourne), South Western (Geelong), Western (Ballarat),

Northern (Bendigo), North-Eastern (Wodonga) and Eastern (Traralgon). Within Central region, two training vacancies were to hand. Unfurling these appointments years on was only due to this publication. Among them some had an immediate or past relationship – Regional Manager Central, David Watson; Regional Operations Manager, Central, John Blackie; Manager Training, Frank Hall; and Manager Manpower Development, Alan Whitla.

> STA inter-office memorandum, dated 7 November 1984 (to me)
>
> Consequent upon the withdrawal of the interview panels first choice Mr D Matthews, and the second choice, Mr B G Freemantle from the position of Regional Training Officer, Central Region, I wish to inform you that the position will be readvertised.
> File 83/3311.
>
> G J Radion, A/staff Officer.

After the readvertisement of the position, Ron Jenkins was appointed as the Regional Training Officer, Central Region. As an interim arrangement commencing 28/10/1984, I was seconded as the acting Operations Training Officer Central Region.

> STA inter-office memorandum, dated 3 January 1985 (to me)
>
> You are transferred from the Personnel & Employee Relations division to the Transport Operations division as Senior

STATE TRANSPORT AUTHORITY – 67 SPENCER STREET

> Training Officer, Operations, (SO1) from 7.1.1985. For seniority purposes, your appointment will be 5.12.1984.
> File 83/3311.
>
> G J Radion, A/Staff Officer.

Just follow the path

My days at Flinders Street had come to an end and my location was now head office, 67 Spencer Street. Two decades plus from my original medical examination and the granite house could be viewed differently. From the pavement, it was a huge monolith that overpowered the space of three quarters of a city block. Symmetrical in shape, the façade divided into five bays. The central bay incorporated the main entrance to four floors with a central corridor running the length of each floor and a basement. Designed in an earlier century, its highlight was the magnificent sweeping stairway linking the ground floor to its next level.

The rooms were high roofed and many cluttered with desk bound multitudes meeting the bureaucracy's planning and administration needs. The chatter of the typing pool was a constant passing their drop off point. Reportedly in an attempt to improve staff morale (1979/1980) the rooms had been completely repainted and the linoleum replaced with carpet. Delighted with a new challenge I was to spend the first weeks with Bruce Freemantle before he moved on. Seconded from Bendigo, from his role of operations officer, he had been impacted by the new regional structures. His expertise in training was as bereft as mine was in rail operational, but not a hinderance to results. Once more a new experience and learning on the run.

Overnight I had moved into training line management rather than the subject matter expert at T&D. My boss was John Blackie and my responsibilities now included locations/centres and instructors of driver, guard, shunter, undergear repairer and conductor training. The infrastructure of training was as varied as the training group with sessional/theory instructors and on-job trainers that covered line sections and routes. Other than subject matter, the difference between technical and operations varied only with the environment. Yet soon I was confronted by the rare exception as I arranged to visit all the sites for training. All the locations had something akin to a classroom where notes and information would be shared before instruction in the yards or siding commenced. This morning it was shunter training for a new group of inductees. I sat in.

We were welcomed and immediately informed that we had entered a dangerous yard location with the continuous movement of trains and shunting moves. Safety was paramount with tons of moving metal and noise. To emphasise his point, our instructor leaned back against a table, dropped his pants and calmly removed his prostatic leg which he banged on the table. His smile was infectious. He had our attention. As my visits continued, I was reminded that operational training and instructors' roles were locked in past agreements. Maybe for another day.

My new home was G17 (or room 17 on the ground floor) which I shared with the Safeworking superintendent and his 2IC. My introduction to Alan Hales and Maurie Diggle was to open the doors to a part of an industry that had paralleled my working life for almost two decades. Maurie freely shared his knowledge of the different Safeworking systems, making my move to rail operations seamless. He also enhanced my operational nous by providing copies of railway accident reports and enquiries from major national systems including British Rail, forensic reports that opened the door to aspects of my new role. Yes, systems failed but the human factor returned time and time again from near misses to incidents. I had worked on many aspects of fixed infrastructure and on many types of rolling stock but never in actual operations. My A grade licence; (no. A8203) so much a motivator of my trade qualifications, was now left in the past.

Although I had always had an ongoing interest in the practice of safety, both personal and risk minimisation, the term 'Safeworking' was specific to rail operations. The blue *Rules and Regulations* book was an early present. These two men were the custodians of the rules and regulations and the decision-makers of all and any new changes. An example, such as Alterations to Regulation 30, would be notified in the Weekly Notice for all operational staff:

> *Regulation 30 has been amended and in its amended form, as shown hereafter, is effective forthwith. 30.(a) No employee under 20 years of age shall engage in any of the following: Inspector, Driver, Guard, Foreman or Ganger followed by instructions for (b), (c), (d)*

Operations training

I was soon to learn that every aspect of operational training was a collaboration with the respective unions. To an independent eye the collaboration was skewed, with decisions dictated by the AFULE or the ARU depending on the work grade. Our first challenge was a temporary complex of portable buildings for the locomotive drivers, located on the city side of the Moonee Ponds creek. The facilities in place, the instructors looked me over as Norm Vukovic, the Driver Training Officer made the introductions. Norm was a committed ex-driver and spanned the gap between the union and operational management. He was an invaluable support as I overviewed the processes and time sequences of training; albeit they were set in stone from years of agreements as technology advanced on infrastructure and working arrangements.

It was soon apparent that each centre had a hierarchical order similar to the apprentice training. The difference was senior instructors in operations had morphed into administrators. My timing was to coincide with major change projects as V/Line sought to introduce freight train operations without guards. This decision had been predicated by the need for rail efficiencies to reduce operating costs and the impact of the overall government deficit. Other workplace efficiencies were planned.

In Western Australia the mining industry had led the way removing the guard and adopting the role in the driver's cab, termed as a second person. Newly introduced technology supported this operation. Alas, any review or potential improvements and insights for guards' training would never eventuate. The proposed new rail operations modes would eventually eliminate these positions. My dealing with Tony Popovic, the senior guard's instructor was robust and cordial, but out of our hands as change drivers would eventually lead the instructor's role to retrenchment or alternative duties. Tony's skills and knowledge would soon be lost to the industry.

Other operational grades such as the shunters would eventually be caught up in these efficiencies. The shunters' instructor Victor Mace was a vigorous advocate of rules and practices and a squeaky wheel to upgraded amenities. Truth be told, Victor would find an excuse to threaten a get-together, from poor air-conditioning to a replacement pie warmer. As the local ARU representative for instructors, we had many discussions under union threat. Work to rules strikes were soon to be part of my normal day.

STATE TRANSPORT AUTHORITY – 67 SPENCER STREET

Bean counters

Somewhere the bean counters were doing their sums and within years the regional structures were under review and destined to fall. The multipliers of administration by five plus were possibly a factor, and not part of my brief. Events were moving with considerable speed. The business of V/line was consolidated to 589 Collins Street and the days of the granite building numbered. The chair of the STA, Keith Fitzmaurice had confirmed that level by level and room by room, 67 Spencer Street after a century or more as the Victorian Railways Head Office would be emptied. Opened in 1893 and vacated in 1985. Forewarned of changes to Central Region, I had applied for a training position at VPC House now the headquarters of the Workshops Division.

> *Inter Office Memorandum. File No: ADP: ED VPC House 17 April 1985.*
>
> *To D Denman, Senior Training Officer. Please note you are the successful applicant for the position of Senior Training Officer at VPC House.*
>
> *Personnel Manager Workshops Division. 2 May 1985*
>
> *Please be advised that after careful consideration I have declined the position at VPC House. D J Denman.*

On reflection, after being advised that I was the workshop's successful candidate, my thoughts of some of its management group said no. Like my A grade licence, my days on the tools were finished.

In the dark corners of the world of administration, my salary increment recommendation was being debated. In a memo confirming the mumbo jumbo of clerical talk is the following dispatch. (Freedom Of Information release)

From Group Manager Personnel, Transport Operations to Regional Manager Operations:

I refer to the memo recommending that Messrs D. Denman and (name removed) progress from SO division 1 to division 3. The position of Training Officer Engineman (Central Region) was recently reclassified at Special Officer 1 without progression specifically to allow for the relativity of the position to the Senior Training Officer (Operations). The classification committee deliberated at length on the relativities of the Inspectors of Locomotive Running, Training Officer Engineman, and Senior Training Officer positions, and it is noted that they did not alter the range of the Senior Training Officer position to say SO 2-4. It is not necessarily anomalous that an employee can report to a person of equivalent salary. Besides in the case of Mr Denman, the Senior Training Officer (enginemen) would normally progress to SO2 and be above the rate of his reportee ... the remaining basis on which a double increment could be considered is for excellence of performance, which the officers are already performing to the maximum attainable level in their positions. However, according to the attached performance appraisals both officers were given an overall assessment rating of 4 or satisfactory. This suggests that both have performed well in their positions and warrant an increment. Accordingly, I approve that D. Denman and (name removed) each progress to SO division 2.

Months later and my passport was stamped for another change.

STATE TRANSPORT AUTHORITY – 67 SPENCER STREET

*Memo to Mr D Denman. Transport Operations Division
                        Room G30.*
Subject: Temporary Transfer 16.10.1985

As from 9.9.85 you are temporarily transferred from the position of Senior Training Officer, Central Region to the Priority Projects Control Department, Level 15, Transport House without change to your classification to assist in Two Man Crewing project.

CHAPTER 14

TRANSPORT HOUSE – PRIORITY PROJECTS

This new location was close at hand and made my relocation a short walk the width of Spencer Street. Owned by the State Superannuation Fund and benefiting with a long-term lease, the arrangement enabled the consolidation of the STA and MTA to its 18-level complex. Another move to another location and an unknown department where my skill set would be challenged again.

I was beginning to suspect that I was the only mug who had a history of training success but without any promotional gain. The occasional head butting with Frank Hall at T&D may have been a factor.

This challenge might open a door

Within days I was linked to the Priority Project Management Control department. The primary function of the department was set out: To provide general direction of projects to meet the corporate objectives established by the project governing body. I was now inserted into project management with Project No 3, Two Man Crewing, promoted by the Chief Operations Manager, John Hearsch.

Level 15 was home to the Priority Projects Control Department headed by Frank Wagner. Frank was reputed to be a commercial heavy hitter from private industry and ran the department with a combination of rewards and threat. His displeasure at times could be heard behind closed doors at a far distance. All projects and the department buzzed with implementing efficiencies that were cost and time driven against budgets and activity progress.

My reporting line on the project chart was to the project manager Alan Dockery. Although half my size, he was a determined operator and an easy person to work with. Alan had runs on the board with operational expertise and the implementation of Museum Station. The throwaway line, where he had been referred to as 'tickety boo' was known only to a few. Alan had prepared the two-man crewing policies and practices manual that provided the blueprint for the task list and the needs of the project. This project had many levels including, planning and engineering (R Roberts), operational design (T Torcasio), Safeworking and operating rules (A Hales) and industrial relations and deployment (B Shaw). This was an insight into a total picture that was rarely upfront in past roles. Denis Leviny was the project coordinator and my direct manager, who over time, I was to find a somewhat remote personality lacking in soft skills. Other than the project, we saw the world differently. He so fitted into that up and down authority structure.

TRANSPORT HOUSE – PRIORITY PROJECTS

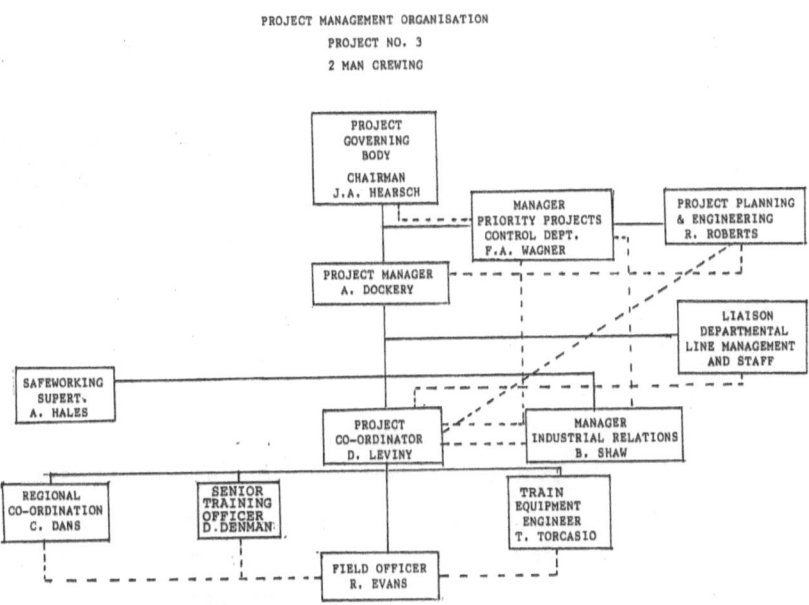

Two-man crewing organisation chart

My brief was to develop the training requirements/documentation for the new freight train operations. Clearly identified and detailed, the role covered a package of needs. It was a brief that was to grow and grow as many pieces of the jigsaw were exposed or came together. Parts of the jigsaw had already commenced, with a working party of ARU and operational instructors overhauling the role and knowledge of the existing guards to transfer and enable the second person role. This working party was the key to the training content and overseen by Robert Evans who was to become an essential confederate.

Victor Mace was another secondment to the working party. Allied to these undertakings, Alan Hales, Superintendent of Safeworking, had been a priority secondment for the new rules. To overview the project, its objective was to implement the operation of two-man crewing on V/line freight trains. To further explain, freight trains normally operated with a train crew of three: an engine driver, a fireman (driver in training), plus a guard at the rear of the train. Train operations skills and knowledge were distributed between the driver who piloted the train, selected routes and responded to signal applications, and the guard who managed the oversight of signals and Safeworking protection where abnormal situations occurred.

An essential part of this implementation was multi-fold including the impact of manpower distribution for training. The workforce training would include drivers, driver's assistants and guards depending on their elected options. Detailed as follows, a guard could elect to train as a second person, enter the driver training scheme or remain in their present classification until this option is unavailable or transfer as a suburban guard. The consequences of these efficiencies would in time affect some country depots, crews and administration and the knock-on status of shunters.

Finally, a link in a team where my skill set and abilities might be an enabler. I had inherited the working party and progressed the flow between Safeworking and training documentation as a priority. My next concern was the selection of instructors who would be the nucleus of our statewide training. Alan Hales and I became the selection panel to determine suitable candidates from current guards. Safeworking knowledge was the mandatory criteria with people and communication skills next in line. On confirmation of candidates, I designed a fit for purpose Train the Trainer course which was presented in the old State Bank premises in Collins Street. Ten good and able candidates were on board and well equipped to meet our role. Practice classes brought on confidence levels and home locations settled for progressive roll outs.

During this period the testing and operation of much of the two-person crew train technical and procedures concluded successfully.

TRANSPORT HOUSE – PRIORITY PROJECTS

Roll by and train separation (break) procedures, including the derogative term of a skinny guard (end of train marker) indicating the last carriage on a train. Progress was steady until an agreement in government to bring the implementation forward. For pawns are seldom consulted but the benefits of team work were soon on show. Training was suddenly in the spotlight as it needed to predate the first train. The operational needs were clear. Sufficient trained drivers and second persons to compliment a grain train between Portland and Ararat. Short of completed documentation, somehow the expression by Frank W, akin to 'if you can't do it, I will find someone who can' didn't really help.

We had contingencies. Infrastructure in place. Portable classrooms had been located into country depots where no suitable options existed (Ararat as a priority location) and drivers rostered for training. My selected instructor was in place and I would support him for his interim sessions. A decision to commence training with the first two days' documentation was agreed while the total documentation was finalised and printed. The many parts of the training gears meshed to meet our timelines. I already had formed a preferential arrangement with the manager of the printing works and he understood our urgency. At 1900 that evening, the photocopier on the 15th floor completed our initial class documentation and notes and I left with all on board in a hire car – next stop Ararat.

In later months, the Western highway was to become a regular route-march as other depots came on line. All was set up early the next morning, documentation in place and our first two-man driver training class commenced. My introduction was clear and the purpose of the training clarified as the early resistance by the driver fraternity to a guard instructor was mollified. We explained the sequence of the program and the role of the examining officers. The local Safeworking inspector would provide the Go/No go result. An agreement with the AFULE stipulated any driver not meeting the standard would be retested. Time constraints may mean alternate Safeworking inspectors being utilised as necessary. One depot commenced, my next implementation point was the enginemen at Dimboola. This location was to provide a couple of hours of distraction when I visited my MURL mentor, Ernie Rudolf and his wife in retirement and distanced from his working life.

Look like

My face was now linked to the voice of help to all of the depot roster clerks as each region came on line. Warmly greeted, without any remonstrations of the advancing changes, they had been instrumental in getting 'bums on seats' at training classes and examinations. My appreciation by word of their juggling act was less than could be acknowledged. For the record, these roster clerks don't fall into the 'all clerks are bastards, but not all bastards are ...'

To many of us a significant date for other reasons, but on 11 November 1985 the first two-man operated train operated between Portland to Ararat. Region by region the training program progressed at their central locations, Dimboola, Ballarat, Geelong, Warragul and Wodonga. The process continued with our guard instructors rotated through centres as they considered their future. My movements around the state coincided with pre-training for dedicated drivers prior to second person implementation.

Decision time

As successive depots became operational and the core of guards acting as second person instructors elected their options, the impact of the project was beginning to bite. The guards who had assisted as instructors now had to make career decisions. As their role in a region completed each moved on to their elected option. Closer to home, we had been tasked with yard working as the second person role was qualified in dividing a train, shunting moves and roles of the guard and or shunter. This involved a shunter familiarisation course of two days class plus instruction in yards and sidings.

We had selected a secondary part of the McCauley rail yard and set up a portable. The yard had adequate track conformation to enable operational working under Safeworking conditions. Next, we rostered (highjacked) an engine and a set of wagons. Victor Mace led this aspect of operations after his period on the working party. At South Dynon, the driver training program continued as guards who had elected to be trained as trainee drivers or second persons were integrated into their program. The various parts of the two-man train operation had seamlessly come together. During this time, I had additionally been part of the central region guard's option selection. There was a degree of disbelief by some guards to these operational changes and a percentage wavered on their decision. On one occasion I witnessed an individual who was clearly in denial and had not elected an option. A member of the panel took his guard's bag and placed it between himself and the panel. She explained: do you agree for you to proceed forward you have to remove this obstacle? The response was a nod. The obstacle of the bag is the same as your problem in electing the option that best suits you and your family. I was witnessing a drowning man who was in need of help. As in many instances of workplace efficiencies, the closure of a depot goes beyond the individual to a wider local community. It is rarely gauged and never entered in the ledger.

Recognition from the top

> *12 December 1985.*
>
> *Dear Denis,*
>
> *I would like to express my grateful thanks for your hard work and dedication as part of the team which successfully developed and implemented the Two Man Crewing Project. As a token of appreciation, I would be very pleased if you would join me at a luncheon in the private dining room, Spencer Street station, at 1.00 pm on Friday, 20 December 1985.*
>
> *Yours sincerely,*
>
> *John Hearsch, Chief General Manager, Transport Operations Division.*

Moving on

As depots came on line, teams of officers, including financial and welfare were meeting with individuals and their family, talking redeployment or surplus to requirements. Some took early retirement, others a retrenchment package. This project had opened the door to restructured grain operations with block trains, train to base radio communication and dramatic reductions in staffing levels with the reform of work practices. Efficiencies came at a cost.

It was an awakening experience for all involved in the project as the numbers game impacted operational needs. Whether this was the

TRANSPORT HOUSE – PRIORITY PROJECTS

State Transport Authority

589 Collins Street.
Melbourne, Victoria. 3000.
Telex: V Line AA33801
Telephone: 619

Reference

12 December, 1985

Dear Denis,

I would like to express my grateful thanks for your hard work and dedication as part of the team which successfully developed and implemented the Two Man Crewing Project.

As a small token of our appreciation, I would be very pleased if you could join me at a luncheon in the Private Dining Room, Spencer Street Station, at 1.00pm on Friday, 20 December, 1985.

Yours sincerely,

JOHN HEARSCH
CHIEF GENERAL MANAGER
TRANSPORT OPERATIONS DIVISION

RSVP   Judy 619 1187
        18.12.85

Two-man crewing completion, 1985

first major success for the Priority Projects Group or not, a day of celebration was placed on notice. Time clouds the actual reason but within a short period, Puffing Billy was booked as our reward and lunch provided at a local pub. Every member of the many projects joined the party. A world away from the environment of Newport Workshops. During this project period a forgotten feedback session with Denis L seemly led to another performance review.

> *To Manager Priority Projects Department, June 23 1986.*
> *The payment of an allowance to Mr Dennis Denman to the level of Senior Officer, (SO) 4 is justified in the context of his responsibilities associated with his secondment … D. Leviny, (erased) Project Manager, Two Man Crew, Implementation. (Source FOI)*

Passenger trains next

The next deployment was the Guard/Conductor review with the objective to operate passenger trains without a guard. Once more Alan Dockery had been allocated the management of this project. Rightful recognition (I hoped) as others were allotted the responsibility for the infrastructure and hardware procurement. Identified as project No 25, my reporting line was direct to Doc, with the responsibility of Training & Manpower. After a two-year stint in Transport House the members of the surviving training team were allocated a shared floor of 600 Collins Street. Bob Evans joined me at 600 Collins Street to continue his role as special officer and operational expert. Our immediate role was to identify the operational changes and establish the training needs and documentation. Once more we were to engage in the process of a working party, negotiating with the passenger guards' team and union.

TRANSPORT HOUSE – PRIORITY PROJECTS

My first success was the secondment of Bob Eddy, a Geelong conductor. Bob was to become an integral member of the team in clarifying the role of the conductor and Safeworking requirements. Other reportees who came on board included Graeme Pack for administration and Trevor Greenwood for input in conductor training. Weeks later a typing temp was allocated. A new team was on board. The Geelong corridor was nominated as the initial trial for this operation as the role of the V/Line passenger guard came under the spotlight. The efficiencies that had been established from freight operations were now sought for passenger services.

The program rapidly came together with my role now moved to team leader and management of any needs analysis of the course programs and on-train training. In broad terms, the conductors' role included, selling tickets as required, ticket checking and passenger control. Additional to these duties any customer interaction from public announcements (PA) to managing disruptions or behavioural issues. The model utilised for freight train operations would now apply to passenger trains with Safeworking protection duties required for abnormal situations and emergencies.

Radio communication between the conductor and the train crew enhanced this proposal. Negotiations continued into our training programs, as a degree of conflict bit the ARU with nominal coverage of both the passenger guards and conductors. I was quickly to learn my way to its then North Melbourne offices with the guard's representative. The two Roberts, Eddy and Evans, were the key to our training success, and they deserve the laurels. Other views on the transitional training deferred but our objectives were in supporting operational changes.

The project moved on and training reverted to the division, as the project team returned to other duties, assuming there were options. Long-term relationships were not part of project work. The two Roberts returned to operational roles, as I vacated 600 Collins Street. Together we had formed a collegiate and successful partnership. In the space of a few years the role of guard had been eliminated from V/line services as the MET considered the guards position on suburban trains.

Six years on from the Cain Government's implementation of the new transport authorities, the rationalisation of the STA and MTA continued at a furious pace. During those years, the Priority Project Control Department was the major driver of operational efficiencies and the 15th floor at Transport House teamed with contractors and seconded V/Line staff. The changes continued under the Joan Kirner government on the retirement of John Cain.

Carriage wash operation

Somehow or other I was steered to Level 16 to report to Graeme Long. Graeme was responsible for the Carriage Maintenance Review and the construction and commissioning of the carriage wash dock/facility. Once more I glimpsed my past as Train Lighting Depot became the scene of the review. Graeme combined the wash plant construction phase with the Suburban Train Maintenance Review. Its purpose was to evaluate future suburban maintenance sites and sidings that would enable the Jolimont Decentralisation Project and the sale of the central rail sidings for commercial opportunities.

Epping depot was developed in the early stage of the project. The team members included Dennis Smith (engineering) who was tasked with the development of new examination sequences and activities, with others involved in the construction schedule plus a clerk of works. My initial role was to review the training needs for

TRANSPORT HOUSE – PRIORITY PROJECTS

the new proposed train maintenance schedules. I was additionally tasked with aspects of the wash dock program. Graeme considered that a salary review for my new responsibilities was appropriate and his recommendation forwarded on the anniversary of my 48th birthday. With the facility completed and contractor staff demobbed, I became the project's de facto commissioning agent.

There was much to do as the carriage wash operation was a push-pull operation on a dedicated road. With agreement of the AFULE on operations, the priority concern was the potential hazard of the cleaning agent. Oxalic acid was an accepted cleaning agent and had previously been used in hand wash operations at the Jolimont wash plant. The difference here was airborne mist overspray on the train crews. In consultation with the corporate OH&S group I arranged testing and airborne reading by Scientific Services. The National Institute for Occupational Safety and Health (NIOSA) provided industry exposure limits and control methods. What a pleasure to liaise again with Bruce Beattie and others from my past at Newport. Beyond his expertise in Scientific Services, his love of steam trains was well known from previous chats. His adventures on steam across the African continent were the tales of boy's own adventures. After numerous tests and notification of accepted international exposure limits the wash dock cleaning process was accepted.

Once more documentation and exposure limitations were presented to the AFULE for a final sign off. Naturally this process occurred over many months and I had inherited the 16th floor and an executive office. Much had happened during my time in Priority Projects and I had finally settled into mature age learning. I had completed the first year of a Graduate Diploma in Risk Management & OH&S as my role moved outside but not exclusively from the training function. With the completion of the 'Suburban Maintenance Review' authored by Graeme Long with major inputs from Dennis Smith, the team moved on. Dennis returned to management in the workshops group, while Graeme accepted a contract from Sydney. Many lessons had been observed during this period including some amusing incidents. A project manager walking out of his boss's office after a progress session become heated. His comment, 'I won't accept abuse from anyone including FW, so, we can continue the discussion once he settles down.' The power byplay didn't work. Win G L.

Tales of seconded regional staff to projects squeezing the living away allowances. Highly paid contractors doing administration and photocopying work as part of their tenure. Efficiencies at any cost and all part of the budget.

The Geelong experiments

Once more (by default) I was attached to the Geelong Yard rationalisation project. The ripple of two-man crewing was now impacting the major rail yards where traditionally train assembly and operations were undertaken by shunters. On occasions, I was to accompany Frank Wagner and Colin Shaw (IR) to Geelong as consultation continued on the sequence of redeployment or the retrenchment package.

The ARU representatives had been extremely effective in supporting the change and adoption of a phased exit. Last on first off, single men before married, those nearing retirement with options of retrenchment. Winners and losers became the norm. This exit strategy would also impact the operations at the grain terminal and 'you can handle that' suggested FW. Lucky me.

Meeting with representatives of the Grain Elevator Board (GEB) placed me front and centre of this new multimillion dollar facility and its rail loop grain acceptance process. The procedure enabled the grain train to be held at a signal before positioning a series of VHGY wagons over discharge pits and the grain to be dropped on an underground conveyer. The process would be controlled by GEB staff that would be trained in hand signals to the train crew and a light signal controlling the initial movement. I had oversight of process and development of the written procedure. The road to the grain elevator site was well worn as armed with the approved Safeworking (Alan Hales) and operational procedures the grain elevator staff were trained to the acceptance of the AFULE and grain elevator management.

Another day, another doorway

My future was detached and this period in projects had seen me last longer than four Transport Ministers: Steve Crabb, Tom Roper, Jim Kennan and Peter Spiker.

To the MET, now formally titled the Public Transport Corporation. Under a personal agreement with building management, I managed to retain my executive office on the 16th floor. In point of fact, I was the sole occupant, as the project team disbanded. Wheels within wheels and a relationship that would by chance be helpful in later years. My view would never be repeated, overlooking the Yarra and Southbank all the way to the bay.

My new role was short term and my business card indicated that I was designated as the Vandalism Control Officer. The job holder had taken three months long service leave. Once more a certain amount of autonomy was at my disposal as other than a weekly meeting to provide incident and frequency reports the role was at my discretion. I took the liberty and approached the job with greater flexibility along with completing my Grad Diploma in Risk Management. My skill base was strongly oriented to the core business of the risk management process models and analysing accidents. I was ever appreciable of the valuable time and case studies that under 'commercial in confidence' were part of my assignments.

With access to a car or occasionally my own I visited most of the stabling sites across the suburban system. The decentralisation project saw the relocation of sets to newly built outer suburb locations and other sites with increased stabling capacity. It was a time that tagging and graffiti of carriages was a social phenomenon. An extract in Met Lines confirms that:

> *Vehicles need to be taken out of service to be cleaned – added to the senseless destruction of ripped seats and damage to repair vandalised station facilities is unclear but estimated to be more that $2 million annually'.*

Offenders (if caught) were being dealt leniently by the judicial system. A designated graffiti cleaning flying squad were continuously servicing the corporate image of transport cleanliness and presentation. During this period, my initiatives had seen the reported incidents increased as a result of greater contact with siding maintenance staff with who records of replaced broken windows and other aspects of vandalism were often missed. Alternatively, my autonomy enabled the flexibility to visit station sidings at shift end. What other idiot turned up at outer suburb sites like Upfield, Ringwood and Glen Waverley station/stabling yards to meet the last train.

The feedback by train crews and station officers stabling last trains were a little in shock. 'We don't see people from head office' was the usual comment, 'or any of their supervisory staff at these hours.'

TRANSPORT HOUSE – PRIORITY PROJECTS

My visits wouldn't change the status quo but indicated the usual gap between head office and remote locations. Rumours that the Wagner regime had run its course were confirmed, yet the legacy of change continued under the new structures.

The success of the two-man operation had invigorated a review of the training of drivers as technology in train operations expanded. Colin Oates who managed the train crew management project was researching simulators and other methods of interactive performance training. Alan Whitla, my time share companion from the bunker had found another home. The AFULE were on board as they saw opportunities in productivity gains and the potential of integration into the new National Public Transport Training Boards national qualifications. Other projects of note include the Dynon terminal centre, CTC train signalling and a universal country train ticketing and booking system. My time chasing vandals was complete as the Graduate Diploma progressed. I now found that my past efforts in efficiencies had arrived at my door.

Public Transport Corporation.   2 January 1992
Mr Dennis Denman,
Train Maintenance and Cleaning Group,
Passenger Train and Coach Operations Department.
Passenger Services Division.

Dear Dennis,
I regret to advise you that your position in the …. has become surplus and you are now unattached. Unattached employees are required to attend a personal interview with a skilled counsellor from the workplace redeployment unit.

Norman Walker, Director
Passenger Services Division.

All clerks are bastards, but not all bastards are ... this expression returned time and time again. Yet in this case the memo had been predicated by a face-to-face chat with Geoff Tighe who had introduced himself as the Personnel Manager. I made it clear that I would seek redeployment and take the opportunity to upskill. During this period, I departed Transport House to relocate to 60 Market Street. Was there any location within this organisation I hadn't placed my jacket? With my past records and recent qualification, I felt reasonably confident of continued employment, in what capacity, I was unsure.

Roll with the punches is an old saying and I had seen the process of dislocation to many individuals from past projects. Others had made difficult decisions. Upskilling was at hand with the opportunity to learn new computer packages and keyboard skills. The days of computer literacy was high on the mandatory role lists and other than my university experience, my day-to-day usage was minimal. The workplace redeployment unit was colloquially referred to as the 'exit lounge'. It was a laissez faire operation with organised learning periods and access to personal computers at other times for the motivated.

The documentation along with its proponents was clear and impersonal. An extract of my job offer signed by the Manager Workplace Redeployment R. (Robyn) F Peterson read as follows:

> *In the event that you refuse the job offer, you will have deemed to have resigned effective from 14 days after the date you should have submitted the job response form (and only receive benefits applicable to resignation). If you believe this offer is not a reasonable one, you may appeal to the Appeals tribunal, C/- registrar at level 14/589 Collins Street, Melbourne.*

TRANSPORT HOUSE – PRIORITY PROJECTS

PUBLIC TRANSPORT CORPORATION

60 Market Street,
Melbourne, Victoria 3000.
P.O. Box 605,
Collins Street,
Melbourne, Victoria 3000.
Telex: AA 151923
Fax: (03) 610 8140
Telephone: (03) 610 8888

7 February 1992

Mr Dennis Denman
Train Maintenance and Cleaning Group
Passenger Train and Coach Operations Department
Passenger Services Division

Dear Dennis

I regret to advise you that your position in the Passenger Train and Coach Operations Department, Passenger Services Division has become surplus and you are now unattached.

I assure you that this decision has not been made lightly and that your previous services have been highly valued by the Corporation.

Robyn Peterson, Manager, Workforce Redeployment Unit will be advised of your position and I suggest you contact the Unit at Level 13/50 Market Street (extension 58182) to discuss your position.

Unattached employees are required to attend a personal interview with a skilled counsellor from the Workforce Redeployment Unit.

If you wish, a representative of your Union may be present at that interview.

If you have any questions in regard to this, please do not hesitate to contact your Divisional/Regional Manager or the Workforce Redeployment Unit.

Yours sincerely

Norman Walker,
Director
Passenger Services Division

V/LINE   Victoria GROWING TOGETHER   The Met.

10267

Letter of surplus, 1992

My brief time in the workforce redeployment unit led equally to a period of self-reflection. The pros outweighed the disbenefits, but my age profile was heading north. I was now in my late forties and outside the formal structure of the authority. The realisation in any workplace is that if you haven't cemented a position by 40 it is unlikely to happen. More so in this industry, where a history in rail operations leads all other criteria. Yet looking about there were many in my view who brought the 'Peter Principle' sharply into focus.

> *'Individuals who perform well in their job will likely be promoted to the next level and continue to rise until they reach the point they no longer perform well.'*
> Dr Laurance J Peter

Once more, all clerks are bastards but not all bastards are clerks. Although, now dated, for the PTC it might be refined to include, 'all personnel managers are bastards but not all bastards are ...'

Obviously, my lens is tainted by this and similar experiences. Prior to the period of my workplace redeployment, I had applied for a position as a coordinator of consultation advertised in the PTC Job Bulletin, in November. On advice that I was unsuccessful, believing my credentials were high, I initiated a normal appeal. Was it my height? Possibly my personality? It was lost in officialdom.

Manager Corporate Support Services, 3 March 1992.

Differences of opinions regarding the appointment to the position of coordinator of consultation… My reading of the relevant section of the Transport Act, indicated the position is an officer of the PTC and subject to terms and conditions of

TRANSPORT HOUSE – PRIORITY PROJECTS

> employment applicable to an officer of the PTC. If this is correct, I believe appeal rights should be available… W J Heywood.

The term 'natural justice' was ignored. I was confounded by a barrier of different responses until all were overridden by the legal opinion of corporate council. The lengths that the system would go to, to keep the status quo was unimaginable. For the record, Bill Heywood was not included in 'all clerk/personnel managers are bastards'.

> *Inter office memo (handwritten)*   *From Geraldine Sharman*
> *6/3/92*
>
> *Bill Heywood, I attach a copy of Section 33 of the Transport Act which governs the standing committee on consultation. Section 33(6) provides that the coordinator shall be approved 'on the nomination' of the standing committee. Section 33(7) provides for a number of matters relating to the appointment of the coordinator such as the term of appointment, remuneration but adds <u>in all other respects</u> be an officer of the corporation. In my view the words 'in all other respects' means that the matters set out in section 33(6) and (7) a-d, overrule the usual terms and conditions of an employee of the corporation so far as these aspects of employment are concerned. In my opinion therefore the appointment to the position … is not subject to appeal because the ACT provides that the appointment 'shall be on the nomination of the standing committee'. If you have further queries …*
>
> *Geraldine Sharman   20/60 Market Street.   (Source FOI)*

C'est la vie.

PUBLIC TRANSPORT CORPORATION

11469

Inter Office Memorandum	Date: 31 March 1992
To:	File No.: KD-DENMAN
MR. D. DENMAN	
LEVEL 9, 60 MARKET STREET	From: REGISTRAR
	PROMOTION APPEALS TRIBUNAL
	KD EXT: 11466 14/TH
	Subject: CO-ORDINATOR OF CONSULTATION

I wish to advise that I note your concerns regarding the Co-ordinator of Consultation advertised in the Public Transport Corporation Job Bulletin dated 6 and 19 November 1991.

I have attached copies of documents, for your perusal, relating to the process taken after the record of interviews was completed, together with a copy of the Act provided in the answer to the advice from Mr. Heywood; and an advice from Mr. L. Conanne, the employment officer handling the file, to Ms. M. Pickworth, Director Human Resources and Industrial Relations.

No indication was given to myself at time of advertising that the proposed appointee from the resulting interview process would not be subject to policy as stated in the Personnel Policies and Practices Manual Section C 2.0 to 2.9 inclusive.

I am unable to comment as to why this was "not disclosed at either employment vacancy criteria, PTC Job Bulletin no 28/91 nor specified or mentioned within the interview process" and I suggest that the you consult employing area and the interview panel for their responses.

REGISTRAR

Coordination of consultation letter, 1992

CHAPTER 15

RESCUED - V/LINE PROJECTS, MET TRAINS & METCARD

Out of the gloom a friendly voice offered a role. On 15 May 1992, I accepted the offer of employment as a Project Officer in the Freight Division, Projects and Administration Department. Passport stamped again, my role was in project support for the rationalisation of freight staffing levels. These reforms were led by the Manager, Projects and Administration, Peter Templer and the seconded team. Peter fitted the term of 'a young Turk' indicating talent and direction. He was a confident and dedicated individual with a natural commitment to his role and the best interests of any displaced individuals.

Reform was almost endemic as the industry confronted occupational rail work grades and trades. The application of new technology in achieving improved operational efficiencies and improved customer service had led the way. Overarching the work of this project was the other State and National Transport industries. The transport industries had recognised severe limitations to their historical operations with inherent classification structures and work types and formed the National Public Transport Training Board (NPTTB). As the industry moved towards single job or classifications, training needs of diversified work would be recognised in terms of a recognised Australian industry qualification (Australian Standards Framework levels). Additional benefits to both the individual and industry would be a portable qualification.

The industry recognised that role and skill sharing might be reached with enterprise bargaining and nationally agreed competency standards. A background player as industrial consultation with multiple unions continued, my skills now extended to the development of generic position descriptions for the recommended work levels. Including the new grades of special electrician, and locomotive power maintenance that would include new electrical skills. I was part of the team at the Industrial Commission hearings and meeting with the peak industry and ETU representatives. Bruce Shaw was the chief negotiator as the corporate IR Manager. Opposite the table at the resolution of the special electrician grade was Gavin Marshall among the ETU representatives. Much had transpired over the years since our mutual time at the ETC. His path from apprentice electrical fitter to an official in the ETU was rapid. He was in later years to distinguish himself far beyond any appointment of a Victorian Railway Commissioner. Dedicated to social and equity reform, Gavin continued his work for the ETU and eventually became a Federal Senator.

Within V/line, Peter Templer had been successful in removing much workplace demarcation and banding work roles at freight centres and country stations. It was 'surely' all about timing and the roles I seemed to find my way to ... structural change, which would once more lead to staff losses as the drive for efficiencies continued.

Outside the fence and a new government turned its spotlight on transport.

After a number of turbulent years, the Kirner Government was comprehensively defeated by the incoming Jeff Kennett Liberal Government. The Hon Allan Brown became the Minister for Public Transport. Six months later and I was appointed as the Manager Training in the Passenger Train & Coach Operations Department. Regrettably my appointment was by appeal against a stations' group insider Lou Costanzo. Lou had been the training officer for station grades including station masters. He was a warm and generous individual who now became unattached. It would seem that my survival was now over the bodies of a few good men. In due course the promotions Appeals Tribunal confirmed that an appeal against my appointment by Mr R Lampre has been dismissed.

> Public Transport Corporation, 19 November 1992
> Inter-Office Memorandum:
> Manager Projects & Administration.
> Mr D Denman, is the successful applicant for the position of Manager Training... Please advise when he can be released to take up his new position.
> L. Meilak, Recruitment & Placement Officer.

Not quite a merry-go round

I could be understandably confused with my new status. Farewell to the V/Line Freight Division and a sort of welcome to the MET, Passenger Services Division that 10 months previous had regrettably listed me as surplus. Within the period of 10 months the swings and roundabouts of a corporation had been exposed. My new home at Level 5, 60, Market Street was led by Pat Kelly, the General Manager Passenger Train & Coach Operations Department, his team consisted of Tighe (Personnel & Finance), Bruce Hughes (Suburban Rail Operations) and Peter Blackman as the Industrial Officer. Once again, under different circumstances my immediate priority was highlighted. Without any reference to our previous conversations (giving me the flick), Geoff Tighe had a problem. His problem was the lease for the stations' training centre that had taken root at Level 6, 152 Collins Street (London Stores) was to expire. One month to find a fix and resettle this group including suburban guards' instructors. Why this lease hadn't been resolved at an earlier period only G Tighe would know.

My introduction was neutral, considering the circumstances of my selection and a directed location change, a replacement manager (me) and disruption to their autonomous lifestyle. Calling on my past relationship with the manager of 'building management' a suitable location was found. The training department was moved into the ground floor, 60 Market Street as part of Passenger Train & Coach. One more part of the jigsaw was also for attention. Out of sight and autonomous were the Safeworking instructors. Set up in FSS, Safeworking classes were an ongoing operational priority, and between classes, a form of correspondence courses were conducted. Relocation as part of the division was gracefully accepted under protest.

RESCUED - V/LINE PROJECTS, MET TRAINS & METCARD

My philosophy was training visibility within the department rather than out of sight, possibly out of mind. That decision wasn't that well accepted by the training group, but a new team was in town. Frank Sutton requested early retirement and Kevin G relocated. During the period prior to relocation, I had sat with each of the guards' instructors to gain insight into 'what they did and how it supported the operational role'. My reaction was somewhere between acknowledging the cultural hang ups associated with various union training agreements and activities that were local and unnecessary. My major concern was the lack of flexibility in the instructional roles as each clung to dedicated specifics, one used full time on producing training aids and presentation slides. My years within 'projects' had developed a hard head for outcomes and flexibility. Regrettably time was ticking as the MET Division courted the role of single person suburban trains. A new training structure and position descriptors quickly followed.

About this time, I produced a 'Future Directions' paper for the Passenger Train & Coach Department. The main headings included an Introduction (the climate), the Transport Reform Agreement (re: the future of training) and an observation of training within the corporation. It detailed the challenges and a detailed course summary of all training grades and occupations. The appendices included suburban guards, V/line conductors, station guards, tram drivers, bus drivers, track and way maintainers, plant and equipment/vehicles operatives, train drivers, Met and V/line, and yard and shunters. Inclusions covered all aspects of Occupational Health and Safety from trauma counselling to dangerous goods. Beyond 'Future Directions' a review of middle managers formal qualifications outside of work-related qualifications led to a live-in weekend development program for senior managers with teamwork objectives and updates of individual department project status. A lot of work to pull it together and never quite sure of the proposed benefits. The feedback was limited.

Although busy with this new role, my progress in completing the final year of the graduate diploma was equally demanding. A major unit requirement was a risk assessment within an industry or commercial setting. With approval of the station management, a risk assessment of the Museum Station services and escalators was confirmed. My partner in this assessment was Alan Duffett, Safety Manager, AOL. We had selected the job hazard analysis technique to identify exposures, potential hazards and control measures to minimise losses. After a site visit and access to the accident reports for the period January 1991 to September 1992, we finalised a report and recommendations. The detailed report under 'in commercial confidence' enabled a successful unit conclusion and forwarded to the Stations Central Business manager. Outcomes: a high credit from Swinburne, no feedback occurred from the stations group.

Other business soon involved an oversight of the driver training proposal for single person operation of suburban trains. I made a number of recommendations regarding time allocations and perceived issues for consultation. A recommendation of own time, paid learning had been floated by the AFULE. After a review combining the session notes and a table top exercise I concurred with the option. All good, but a reminder it was a under the driver project remit so my role was confirmed as manager training but not drivers. Seems I could be used for independent reviews when needed.

Significant technology was embraced as part of the suburban train operation with CCTV aiding the driver where stations with curves unsighted the rear unit and radio communication and mobile phones issued as part of one person operation. Others were busy within the Driver Only Project, managed by John Anderson as a risk analysis of train operations was detailed. The brief from the PTC detailed a study through a working party including AFULE representatives with the necessary input from Viner Robinson Jarman Pty Ltd, consulting engineers who had completed a 'risk' analysis associated with the role of radio communication in driver-only train operations. They wrote:

> *This report responds to the letter from the AFULE dated 25 August 1992 and also includes consideration of the areas of further work included in our letter of 13 August 1992. Additional sensitive analysis has been carried out and the results for the various options are compared in terms of risk reductions achieved per dollars spent. The report concludes that the combination of short term and longer-term Driver Only Project initiatives will provide a significant decrease in risk compared to the current two person operations. (Source: Consulting Risk Engineers, 4 Sept 1992).*

The first driver-only trains commenced running in 1993, coinciding with my graduation ceremony.

News release

17 March 1993, 09:53am. Bigger wheels were turning as the Minister of Transport sent the following fax to the Chief Executive of the PTC:

Historical rail deal for Victoria. Public Transport Minister Alan Brown today announced an historical railway deal that will deliver Victoria a world-class transport system. Mr Brown said he had agreed to a memorandum of understanding that meant the government, Trades Hall and Public Transport Unions would work together to conduct the most sweeping reforms ever of Victoria's

ONCE UPON A TRAIN

MINISTER FOR PUBLIC TRANSPORT

NEWS RELEASE

CB
WV
EDN
PB
GT

HISTORIC RAIL DEAL FOR VICTORIA

Public Transport Minister Alan Brown today announced an historic railway deal that will deliver Victoria a world-class transport system.

Mr Brown said he had agreed to a memorandum of understanding that meant the Government, Trades Hall and public transport unions would work together to conduct the most sweeping reforms ever of Victoria's transport system.

The agreement was reached after six weeks of intensive negotiations involving Mr Brown in 14 rounds of talks with Trades Hall representatives and the PTU, ETU, AMEU, PGEU, ASU, FIMEE, APESA, ARPOA and the CFMEU.

The four year agreement between the Government and the public transport unions demonstrates a commitment to the operation of the Public Transport Corporation at international best practice levels of efficiency and performance.

Mr Brown said he had succeeded where the previous Labor Government had failed miserably -- the implementation of real reform of the public transport system with industrial peace.

"The deal is good news for both Victorian public transport users and taxpayers," he said.

"It saves most rail services while at the same time dramatically reduces the financial burden on Victorian taxpayers.

"The Government will still be able to achieve its savings of $245 million a year through work practices reforms that will reduce over-staffing in many areas of operation.

"The public transport unions have also agreed to microeconomic reforms that will see rail passenger and infrastructure services operated on an international best practice level.

"We deserve a world standard of public transport in Victoria and can now obtain it after decades of waste and mismanagement.

"Driver-only train operation and automated ticketing, with changes to station staffing and the introduction of roving customer services employees, will be phased in over an 18 month period.

.../2

Minister's 'news release'

transport system. the agreement was reached after six weeks of intensive negotiations involving Mr Brown in 14 rounds of talks with Trades Hall representatives and the PTU, ETU, AMEU, PGEU, ASU, FIMEE, APESA, ARPOA and the CFMEU...

Other features of the agreement include: the government guarantees to retain rail passenger services on at least six country corridors. Four are guaranteed to be operated by the PTC, but up to two could be operated by private sector operators.

The unions have agreed to micro-economic reforms aimed at achieving taxpayer savings in the workplace and freight areas.

Rosters will be changed for a reduction of up to 50 metropolitan electric train drivers. Item 9. Training of PTC staff in all aspects of Safeworking will be retained in-house. <u>All other training could be contracted out</u>. (Note: the full text is not recorded here.)

From a system to a service

In January 1993, the government announced its public transport reform strategy 'From a System to a Service', and the goals of the reform package were spelt out clearly. Public transport would be: clean, safe, reliable and cost effective. The strategy had two main elements. The first was largely achieved, with the biggest ever reduction in the transport deficit in a single year. This reduction amounted to a saving of $97 million when compared to the 1992/93 year.

The second element, providing quality services, commenced in March 1994, with clear service performance targets set for the Public Transport Corporation's train, tram and bus services. Somewhere around this period the PTC devolved into business units with responsibility of discrete transport functions. Some bus lines were sold to private operation. The rail and tram operation were separated to become Met Trains and Met Trams. Met Trains was the rail component of the Passenger Train & Coach Operations. Suggested as a correlation between the division not meeting government performance standards and Pat Kelly moving to A Goninan & Co. was speculative.

Naturally this major change didn't immediately rock the wheels of the Passenger Train & Coach Operations or my performance review. Tighe in full flight with the warmth of a bean counter, noted the following:

> Dennis has been in position for 12 months. Difficult times taking over from an incompetent manager, staff with limited skills in training, staff exodus on account of VDP/TSP and uncertain corporate environment. Work on a needs analysis has not progressed sufficiently quickly and staff management is an area of concern. Perhaps Dennis needs to review his approach. I have arranged for him to attend Myers-Briggs which should give him insight to his personality. He needs to plan ahead in more detail, upskill or shed staff and pump-up productivity rate from training. (Source FOI)

Events were to intervene but an independent observer might wonder who was on the original selection panel (incompetent manager reference) which would normally include the position's manager. Once again possibly an example of the function of training disconnected from executive management other than an outcome and a cost. The Kennett government's position was clear.

Met Trains and Transport House

For the second time I was to become a resident within Transport House. The building (with the exception of a couple of floors) was the modernised head office with all its operational modes. Access was open and laissez faire with minimal controls to enter the building and proceed to a nominated floor. Building security during this period had not been high in assessing risk. Like the times, this was to change.

November of 1993 saw the release of the organisational chart for Met Trains. The so-called international executive search had conferred a Pom. Simon Lane had been headhunted as the managing director. Three senior group managers and an appropriate tier of function managers formed the executive team. Once more my progress was to be uncomfortable as I had to reapply for the training manager's position.

Here we go again

Considering my views of fairness and the impact of redeployment, another challenge was at hand. With the suburban trains progressing their driver-only program, my legacy to the role of guard was unfortunate, the wrong place at the wrong time. I had been part of efficiencies that removed every guard from the rear of a train. The guard instructors in most case exited the industry.

The executive team had changed some faces. Tighe had moved as the GM of V/line passenger trains. Peter Blackman was now the personnel manager and my manager (a note in the *VR Newsletter*, July 1967 reported Peter who along with a P Turner were one of the first national servicemen to complete their training and return to the department) and Bruce Hughes, Group Manager, Operations. Met Trains had inherited the component of coach and station services and their training group, so in effect, there was two candidates for the manager training position. Another interview process and selection process leading regrettably to someone else being unattached.

Brains trust, Met Trains personnel, 1997. P Blackman (left) D Denman (centre) V Dalinkiewicz (right)

I was beginning to feel my age. I could never be assured of fair and without favour but the memo confirmed my appointment. The other applicant was Warren Frehse who left shortly after for a successful career as an author and transition expert. Redeployment and redundancy packages were back in vogue.

The training department was realigned to a new structure that picked up the initiatives of customer service employees, station grades and Safeworking. My first priority was a training audit of staff skills/qualifications and current course programs. Following was our capacity to meet new projects aligned to identified or potential business needs. I was somehow stuck in the middle of circumstances that had seen me realign a second training department within two odd years. Some redundancies followed and after selection interviews I confirmed other appointments. I had inherited an enclosed office and a new clerical assistant, Nevenka, and a group of some half dozen training officers. Evicted from the office soon after as the 15th floor was refurbished to an open space work area with window offices reserved for executive staff. The open floor plan divided each area by work function and the training and management services groups separated by a passage and shoulder height partitions. The design was somewhat like a maze with connecting portals. Each workstation (desk and computer) was arranged one behind each other. But ...

Vive la difference

As my workspace had two partitions at right angles opened on one side by the throughfare, I configured my workspace to a different layout with my desk and PC facing a wall and a round table between myself and the next work station. This layout gave me two separate working spaces, desk and table, with the latter a neutral area for formal and informal discussions. This layout worked particularly well between my group and visitors as it took away the power relationship that a manager holds from behind his desk. A message not understood by my peer managers without my need to explain. Yet to my amusement, it became a stirring pot for many.

There were new relationships to form and clarification of our role and reporting to the needs of the business unit. Some hesitant, some carrying scars from our previous group. From P.T.& Coach, Safeworking instructor, Kevin Giovannini, ex-guard's instructors, Gino DiNiro and Derrick DiSilva joined Abraham Caljouw, Alan

Easter and others. Alan was well known in theatrical circles for comedic roles and TV commercials. Sometime later, Christina would be highjacked from the stations group where, as a qualified teacher, she was working in Metrol after commencing as a station assistant. Well found Peter B, who naturally took credit.

There was much to do as the Kennett government released their mid-term report. History would record that cost reduction in public transport had become a necessity with operating deficits in real terms $488 M in the year 1992/93. (Source: Mid-term report. Hon A Brown August 1994). By 1993/94 Victoria's transport deficit was a major drag on the government's budget. Initiatives by the MET (tram division) in the early nineties had seen the introduction of scratch tickets and paralysing subsequent strikes. It was now Met Trains turn for greater efficiencies and cost reduction.

At the pointy end, the new business unit was involved in multiple government initiatives as well as operating a cost to revenue conscious service. Met Trains' basket would become near to overflowing as efficiencies and decisions of government swept in the door. Major priorities included the Jolimont Yard relocation, Federation Square and roofing a section of the FSS yard. The relocation of Metrol and Electrol. The Flinders Street Station redevelopment. Automatic ticketing, single-person suburban train operation, and the introduction of Customer Service Employees (CSEs). Other national drivers included the Public Transport Corporation participation in the National Public Transport Training Boards start up in work group task identification. Here I had a head start as my involvement in the freight projects was recent and relevant to work groups reform. Freight service were ahead of the curve with work grade multi-skilling and enterprise bargaining. I had plenty of options to pick from and many masters. My role was now to blend the training group to the new initiatives of Met Trains.

Where to start

The juggling act commenced. Training facilities. With a free hand I approached my friendly and helpful building management. As the 14th floor was vacant, would that be suitable? Within the month my floor design was accepted. With Blackman's approval the wheels spun into action and a training facility completed. Walls installed, air conditioning and service systems modified and connected. I had a free hand as Peter was busy with the new CEO's induction and always had his eyes in that direction. We progressed two dedicated rooms for training or management presentations, two smaller rooms for syndicate working, a resourced kitchen and recreation/meal room. A short time later, a fully integrated Premier Station Control desk and all its functions was installed. In essence, we had a working simulator of all the functions of the operators control and communication systems. Designated by the acronym, the PRIDE (Passenger Realtime Information Dissemination Equipment), computer, closed circuit television monitors and public address facilities was linked to the platforms. We were to commence training station staff along with the automatic ticket equipment to meet the proposed roll out on the Alamein line.

Managing the engineering and equipment rollout for AT equipment was Bob Roberts. Bob was a friendly an amenable individual and soon become an ally as we had common outcomes to meet. Our paths had crossed previously from Priority Projects in similar roles. He arranged for me to meet with ERG (OneLink) supplier management team and visit the supply factory. With agreement from OneLink (automatic ticketing contractor) this dual training activity commenced with one of each of the automatic ticket vending and validating machines made available. These machines were installed separately in an area of our training facility. Met trains now had a dedicated home for all training including Safeworking, customer relations employees and station staff.

In some ways I operated in my own little bubble reminiscing of the major project days. I had access to all the pieces and timelines with little need of my line manager. Regular progress reports hit his desk weekly. Still bigger fish were on the CEO's boardroom table. My balancing act was to bring the training of the user groups together at the right time. The primary purpose of the CSEs was initially to be hosts for the introduction of the automatic ticketing. It was envisioned that these CSEs would be riding all three transport modes and helping passengers with information. Unfortunately, in my view as they were managed by the revenue protection department of the stations group, it would eventually lead to role confusion … but that was for another day. So, establishing the relationship of the automatic ticketing and the role of the CSE, our training schedules could be planned to lead the rollout time lines. Testing of the Metcard and the prototype ticketing machines was ongoing for various user groups, including those with special needs. This type of card was to replace the existing tram and train paper ticketing systems and the ill-fated scratch ticket, and in the case of trams, be a step towards removing conductors. As a universal mode ticket, its eventual advantage was availability at nominated locations beyond the traditional station or tram. It was proposed that they could be pre-purchased at various locations including small retail shops.

The training triumvirate

With all transport modes in play – tram, bus and train – the training managers of each mode initiated a regular meeting where issues of similar employee grade and services were mutual. This successful initiative grew to greater advantage as the NPTTB's workplace task analysis gained impetus. Each transport mode had been tasked to set up working groups to identify the tasks and competency standards of nominated employment occupations. Employment groups would be defined as career streams with occupation rail examples, such as train crews, train controllers, station employees, and corporate to include, finance, human relations and administration.

A regular series of meetings was timetabled for this informal group to review training matters and the respective modes NPTTB project progress. With changes to the CSE training program (train) introducing the benefits of accredited trainers was now a necessity. The flexibility of our trainers to meet our 'project like' challenges was now confirmed.

My review of the content had refined the training to blocks of product knowledge, service knowledge and informational/conflict resolution. Elements of feel-good visits to locations were removed. After a month at their workplace another two-day training block and feedback was initiated. Total training time reduced, without any loss of effectiveness. ARU advised by letter: one objective met. Unfortunately, the exchange of learning and competency attainment options were soon minimised as restructures impacted each business unit.

Staff development

Progressively, each training officer completed the 'workplace training' module as an accredited trainer with a private provider. To add capacity and flexibility, Nevenka also completed the module. The PTC had (since corporation) been swept along embracing terms and practices of 'world best practice', 'accredited safety' (National Safety Council of Australia), and 'performance measurement' in all aspects of its business.

During this period, knock-on activities from operational projects found their way to my desk. The suburban driver's agreement specified the delivery of public address announcements. My previous experience of drivers' responses to guards' instruction in V/Line's two-man crewing was still fresh. Their initial attitude collectively was poor but most were open to change. My challenge to Christina and Nev was to provide practical public address training for drivers. As the driver's depot was adjacent to Batman Avenue, an agreement for access to Princes Gate was concluded. The bunker, now rarely used, became the venue for suburban drivers' PA training. We had written 'corporate' messages and the opportunity for freestyle messages to assist the learning process to the new role. Taped feedback provided group reinforcement. I made it a point to introduce both women for the first few sessions to send a message of acceptable behaviour. This was new ground for an all-male driver industry and their acceptance of the skills and roles of two attractive young women. Not part of their feedback, but they confirmed there was always a few arseholes within the ranks. Female train drivers where not to hit the network for decades.

The utilisation of the bunker was as it should have always been. Sessional class, then lock up and leave. Parallel with single-person train operation was the introduction of premier stations. Every operational function was being stressed, with technology change and training as the common link.

Happy birthday

My birthday in 1994 sees the number five lead my age. The previous year had flown, with positives abounding with a little socialisation. The weight of AFL and the continued chatter of every football sport between Blackman and Viktor Dalinkiewicz (Manager Human Services) was the food of the personal group. Simon Lane was not impervious, as they added soccer and international rugby to the daily review. I had joined the duo and their families at occasional MCG night matches. The Western suburbs and the Western Bulldogs were their mantra. With an engaging smile, Viktor's day role had been widened as the nominated chief warden for the floor deserving of a hard hat and torch. The piercing chime of the emergency warning system was to see the steady exodus of every floor via the stairs. The higher your floor, the more the knee joints rang as we were shepherded to our assembly point. Viktor was the chief shepherd as he ushered the slow ones towards the stairs. Another opportunity for a stir.

Beyond the walls of Transport House, my surviving parent was having health issues. The management of the building risk had turned full circle. Yet I needed food beyond sport and distractions of other types and applied for a Diploma in Education & Training. I commenced the following year.

Not all went to plan

My mother who was previously able to maintain a happy and comfortable independent life, now underwent periods in and out of hospital. As her only dependent, decisions on her future living arrangements become my priority with the world of business secondary. Thanks to some flexibility in my role, the search for placement and care began.

Who, when and how

We now had a flexible workgroup and an ability to respond to the various needs. We were busy, and juggling resources became a major time consumer. Christina had married changing her name from Pesos to Semple. Together with Abe she had commenced the progress of multiple CSE classes before beginning the Onelink adventure. Her background in station work placed her ideally to initially learn the station working for automatic ticketing sales and the validating equipment. Enter Victoria Baldwin-King, OneLink representative, to take us through the operation of the fixed AT equipment. A Train the Trainer program was conducted by Ms Baldwin-King and Helen Berman from AES Prodata at the Met Trains training facility for Christina, Kevin and myself. We would follow on and train our team members as required.

Slowly, the build-up of priorities began to bite as the different parts of the many came together. Derrick and Christina for CSE training, and as Derrick's capacity grew to become our control desk guru. Regrettably, during the height of our demands, Nev approached me with personal concerns indicating she would have to resign. Any possibility of a redundancy would help. Someone agreed and with our blessing another face disappeared. The note was unexpected.

> *Dear Dennis, thank you for everything and especially for your support through my tough times. I wish you the best for the future. Nevenka.*

RESCUED - V/LINE PROJECTS, MET TRAINS & METCARD

UPDATE ▶ ISSUE 3

The Key to Melbourne

Training the Trainer

Training has been progressing well in the last few weeks. A 'Train the Trainer' education program has been completed to give trainers the knowledge they need to train our PTC operational staff across all three modes of transport.

Training for Met Tram and Met Train was conducted in a special facility at Hawthorn Depot and Transport House in Collins Street respectively. Bus training will take place at individual Depots, using portable boards set up with a Validator and Ticket Issuing Machine.

All the equipment necessary for Phase I implementation in your working area, will be at the training facility. For example, the facility for Trams included: Metcard vending machines, Metcard validators, a Depot Computer System and a Portable Ticket Reader.

Staff were given the opportunity to ask questions about any aspect of the equipment and its use.

The people who have attended 'Train the Trainer' have been helping to draft procedural manuals for staff use. The manuals are

Train the trainer in progress with (l to r) Victoria Baldwin-King (OneLink), Kevin Giovannini (Education Officer, Training Group, Met Trains), Christina Semple (Education Officer, Training Group, Met Trains), Helen Berman (AES Prodata), and Dennis Denman (Manager, Training Group, Met Trains).

designed to help you to integrate AT into the things you do every day.

To make sure that all modes of transport communicate effectively, a Training Working Party has been established across the three modes. The Training Working Party is looking at information you will need to know when advising customers on changing modes of transport during a journey.

Includes
▶ Training the Trainer
▶ Telling Our Customers About the Benefits of AT
▶ Getting to Know: Portable Memory
▶ Field Trials Underway

Telling our Customers about the Benefits of AT

Communications material, which will be used to tell people about the introduction of AT, has been tested for public feedback. Research was conducted using focus groups of users to evaluate the effectiveness of the advertisements and brochure.

Group discussions took place involving people who represented key users of public transport. These people were shown copies of the AT advertisements and public information brochure.

Overall, the feedback was very positive and key recommendations from the focus groups have been used to fine tune the communications materials.

Metcard information sheet

207

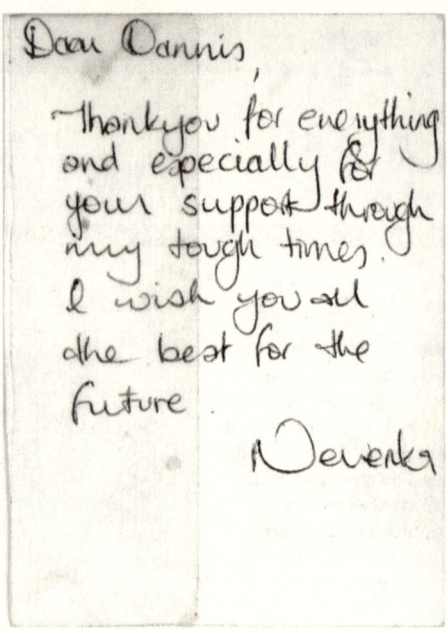

Nev's letter

Managing up and managing down

The basic building block of communities and certain workplaces might include; where we are now and how we are going. Managing up were Peter's personnel groups' meetings where progress was noted and methods of progress provided. Usually lightweight and sociable. A period brief supported by charts indicating total population, percentage completed, numbers outstanding became the norm. I don't recall any comments referring to the move beyond Met Trains or to privatisation, his meetings usually concluded with rumours and what Simon is doing as he met with government. Managing down was a little more confronting as the penny hadn't dropped for a few.

Gino as the ex-guards ARU representative was under the misapprehension that past activities should still be relevant. He felt they should maintain their past time roles, starting at 7.30 and finishing at 3.30. An exercise of costs including our salaries, superannuation and overhead, that would buy significant private training was sort of lost in translation. As my insight to the group's motivators increased, it reinforced that each of us had lives outside this 9 to 5 regime and these sometimes came into conflict. Such as other forms of income or childminding and in my case a parent's illness and care. My meeting's objective was to provide assistance in their roles and to enable each to know the progress of others. Our social lives rarely came together.

The CSE training format allowed Derrick to support Abraham with the overlap period and add flexibility to our resources. There was some division in the ranks for a higher rate of pay, but without my support, we agreed to disagree.

Feedback

No-one was excluded from my oversight in their course presentation including Gino and Kevin on Safeworking. Course feedback information doesn't tell all the picture. We called them 'happy sheets'. I had from day one of our CSE training presented a communication session during the course. A surprise to the ones I met at their selection interview. For a period, I was part of the selection panel. There is a particular pleasure in sharing information that occurs between a trainer or teacher and this opportunity to develop a relationship with a trainee. With adults, the importance of this interchange is understanding the life experiences and knowledge they bring to the process. A tenet for everyone involved in training not to forget. I was additionally pleased that our CEO managed to drop in for a five-minute visit at almost every CSE course. Simon practised what he preached. Management visibility. But it was not always to be my experience.

Opportunity knocked, sort off

Whether my timing was right for the business or my ego got in the way could be argued, but no-one did. The larger picture presented by the NPTTB was clear that future training would be accredited for all aspects of the transport industry. After all my charter wasn't running the business, but providing trained and qualified staff was. The intent was to add a number of suitable accredited modules of the certificate in workplace education to the customer service employee's course. To deliver vocational education and training required an application to the Office of Training and Further Education. Subsequently a submission in late 1995 to OTFE was made successfully. The Met Trains, a business division of the Public Transport Corporation of Victoria was granted accreditation by the State Training Board of Victoria to present the following licensed certificates:

- 3222DGB Certificate in Workplace Leadership
- 2005AEB Course in Workplace Assessor (Hawker de Havilland)
- 2112.2112ADC Certificate I in Workplace Education
- 2212ACC Certificate II in Workplace Education
- 2312A Certificate III in Workplace Education.

The modules would be purchased from the Gordon Institute of Technology in Geelong. This decision was agreed to, but went through to the keeper as senior management had more pressing issues. A letter of agreement from Gordon Institute confirmed we (Met trains) could deliver selected modules which could be integrated into the CSE course. Competency-based training had arrived by stealth to employees of Met Trains.

Computer-based training

An opportunity to commence computer-based learning for non-driver grades was linked to the V/Line driver training. In past years they had cemented a training facility at South Dynon and contracted a driver simulator. Its purpose: to derive efficiencies in the training timelines. Allied to this contract was a computer-based program that would replace aspects of face-to-face time. Learning could be undertaken independently by a trainee by selecting alternative or multiple-choice answers to a developed lesson. With their background in Safeworking systems, I arranged with their agreement for Kevin and Gino to work at South Dynon and develop an option for signals and Safeworking systems. They were inducted into the program locally and settled at South Dynon with high expectations. A straight shift was the trade-off, the catalyst for efficiencies in training drivers with the use of best practice technology, including a simulator and computer-based options.

The imperative to the AFULE in their agreement to these efficiencies long term, could be assumed to retain a perceived parody to a tradesman rather than a skilled machine operator. Accurate or not, but a point of view. Historically a fireman on a locomotive (steam, then diesel) spent five years, sometimes much longer, on the footplate awaiting a vacancy before being eligible as a locomotive driver. The AFULE was always about status and income maintenance with a need of an accreditation for a ASF Level 4 then Certificate IV. Driver training had once more crossed my desk but this time in the guise of a status review of the South Dynon training centre and its commercialisation brief for privatisation. Along with Peter, I attended a meeting convened by Walter Whitburn who was managing this aspect of the computer-based learning system. The meeting included Wayne Walsh and Bruce Hughes from operations and Alan Whitla from projects. A rare get together.

The key confirmations were that Fujitsu was reworking the system under warranty. It was planned for installation of a number of computer stations (8) at Flinders Street Station. Two Met training staff (Kevin and Gino) were currently developing CBT lessons for Safeworking, confirming my earlier placement decision. GEMCO training involves four expert simulator instructors to carry out the Instructor/Driver role. The Met simulator was utilised each day for driver training, with the V/line simulator only in use for remedial or continuation training. The Ministry of Transport opinion that the Training Centre be either commercialised or outsourced had not changed. (Source personal papers).

The winds of change continued and other than cursory exchanges my involvement with driver training ceased other than social visits. I retained links to various instructors who were undertaking Higher Education courses of which we had previously agreed would assist them in their role. I signed the content course approval (external studies) and Victor D authorised the fees reimbursement.

Top down

Sometime within this period Simon Lane directed two major business decisions relating to management development and systems. Both decisions that might have had my input, but handled directly by Peter and Simon. Conjecture on my behalf but it seemed that Peter had become Simon's aide-de-camp, beside his day role of personnel manager. He had obviously undertaken some spade work to find an organisation that could provide a module system of management training. My first input was accompanying Peter to Malvern, possibly the Melbourne Institute of Business. Every manager would be offered the opportunity to undertake core modules as part of a formal qualification. The modules would be undertaken on a day release and any cost reimbursed via the staff development budget.

The program overview was positive and the first intakes commenced at the following semester. The other program was a system program run in-house by the contractor where core functions would be identified and analysed by designated teams. These teams would comprise membership of key stakeholders and others with method input. The program was top down with senior managers selecting teams that would then complete a business outcome. The program had been developed to enable the end product or recommendation to become integrated into the specific department. Incident and frequency measurements underpinned the program. Every team would present their findings and recommendations to the senior management group. The impact of teamwork and measurement became the catchphrase of Simon's tenure.

I had been nominated to lead a team into a review of the Metrol controllers but withdrew for personnel reasons due to my mother's continued health issues. They weren't happy. I had additionally been placed in a team that was to design and recommend a process for staff appraisals. Led by Viktor D this appraisal format was successfully completed and implemented. A win for our group, yet not so dissimilar from the format of the past disaster of T&D, but then they didn't have that memory. Viktor, with his gregarious personality was the hub of the floor in providing light relief. He was a perfect foil to my quieter brand of interaction and the target of my occasional stir.

Different role for other levels as updates to the Microsoft packages necessitated a steady stream, including trainers uptown to learn the next Microsoft update. At the time I believe IT training was a contract arrangement between the Victorian Government and Drake Training. A pleasant day or two interludes as the training occurred in the Sofitel on Collins Street. Included in the training was sumptuous catered sandwiches of the highest order and for the male of the species the opportunity to piss at a urinal with a view overlooking the MCG parklands.

Moving on

My involvement with the NPTTB was increasing as the different groups within Met Trains were identified and the members of working parties selected. A presentation by the CEO of the NPTTB had provided a clear picture of the objectives and information for the overall transport industry and specific work groups allied to the Public Transport Corporation. The overall coordination for the PTC was the Corporate Workplace Department, with Met Trains to manage the working parties for station operations and management, customer/passenger service operations and coordination with V/Line freight for locomotive train driving.

The call for membership was quickly established and I took responsibility for the working party to establish the passenger service standards. Successful liaison with Trevor Greer, manager of Stations & Revenue, enabled the release of experienced staff. The membership covered operatives across the spectrum of work grades and their roles. Over the coming months a forensic audit of all tasks associated with passenger services was itemised and listed. The list was then arranged in a sequence of order, before establishing competency levels from entry levels to advanced.

The balancing act continued between personal and workplace needs as the latest health issue of my mother became the priority. I had recommended Christina to add her input to the passenger service working party. Beyond this task and competencies identification, was the role of drafting generic workplace level descriptors of which I had already completed Level 1. With the NPTTB offering a three-day seminar for transport members Christina became the obvious participant ... talent as well as competence saw her Sydney-bound to our mutual benefit.

Leave of absence

My search for a suitable care facility for my parent was urgent. Her recent period in hospital had led to this recommendation which was concluded at week's end. Comfortably settled, I could now return to the issues at Transport House. The suburban system by this period had implemented single-person suburban train operation and a number of premier stations had been identified and commissioned. The introduction of Metcard and automated ticketing was gathering pace and consequently the training of station staff and other grades increased.

Lighter moments

There were lighter moments, and after a week's leave I returned to the odd smirk and a cheery hello as I entered the floor. Surprise, surprise, my work station had been repositioned to meet the hum-drum of conformity ignoring my personal requirements. Out of character and with their entertainment to be considered my reaction was over the top including expletives. Within the hour, all was reinstated and humour restored. On my desk had been a welcome note and a pager. It remained in the drawer. Not long after, I arranged for a technician from IT to connect a spare computer into the training floor. I had organised a bolt hole with total privacy away from distractions of the 15th floor. Not even the CEO had a second private office.

Communication continued to impact every aspect of the business. Driver to drivers and train control and station control centres – everyone was in the loop. In previous projects Motorola had been the contract supplier for train radios that extended to mobile phones as suburban train operation moved to single-person operation. There was an entrepreneur in the building, let's call him George. With his contacts in communication, he proposed that a mobile phone with a competitive plan could be purchased if we contracted a bulk buy. With the support of AFULE numbers, over 2000 signed on the dotted line. The personnel group were among the fortunate. An avalanche of phones arrived on our doorstep. Many had purchased additional units for their family, my count plus one.

It was but a pleasant distraction to the day-to-day pressure of business, as the impress of efficiencies were imposed on each department. Senior department managers were to find 2% productivity increase, 2% reduction in costs and 2% reduction in manpower. At a combined managers and staff meeting, progress on the government's mandate and the suggestion that half of the numbers in that room might not be here in the future was a sobering thought. With a number of balls in the air I missed the cues as distractions increased.

Personal development

With the Education & Training Diploma well underway, and with units either at night or on weekends, I was busy. Initially controlled by the Hawthorne Institute of Education it was to be consumed by the Melbourne University. With my work experience I had been able to seek credits in a few modules but found that my previous roles in project management and structural reform put me far in excess of some lecturer's brief. On structural reform I was able to provide a perspective of the transport industry on a national scale. Not so on the 15th floor where my previous qualification was unknown or ignored, my appointment was as training manager, and the reason to seek another qualification. In hindsight I might have thought about an MBA, but at my age, this time my qualification would be paid for by the PTC. I now became the complete resource manager and used my time and aspects of work-related experiences and projects as themes for written papers and presentations (submitted to the university under commercial in confidence).

My time with NPTTB had run its course as the stations operations project completed its packaging and referencing phase. The following letter indicated the status of station operations:

Public Transport Union – Australian Rail, Tram & Bus Union
21 April 1997 to Dennis Denman – PTC. Lindsay Carter – QR, Nick Serminidis - ASU

Please find attached drafts of levels 3, 4 and 5 of the station operations group. There are some errors in the documents that I have identified namely ... on completion, would you please review this and let me know if it accords with your records. Yours sincerely,
Andrew Thomas, Assistant National Secretary (Rail Operations Division).

ONCE UPON A TRAIN

NATIONAL PUBLIC TRANSPORT TRAINING BOARD
7TH FLOOR, 140 WILLIAM ST
EAST SYDNEY NSW 2011

Ph: (02) 356 2311
Fax: (02) 368 1308

DENNIS DENMAN
MANAGER, TRAINING
MET TRAINS
LEVEL 12, 589 COLLINS ST
MELBOURNE VIC 3000

Dear Dennis,

RE: COMPLETION OF PROJECT 6

On behalf of the Chairman and the Board, I would like to thank you for all the time and effort that you have put into the Passenger Services standards, particularly in the last stage of validation and signing off the documents. I know this has taken up a great deal of your energy over the last few months, and the outcomes would not have been anywhere near as good without the committment of the Working Party members.

The documents themselves were brought to us by NCVER, and it appears that mainly due to the solid work done in earlier stages of the project, most of the final comments involve some terminology changes only.

Copies of the final standards will be given to your Board members for distribution in February.

Again, thank you for your help with, and committment to the project.

Your sincerely,

SALLY-ANN THOMAS
EXECUTIVE DIRECTOR

11 December 1995

Ref: KU\Projects\Project 6\PU_04DEC.doc

NPPTB, Project 6 completion, 1995

The NPTTB had finalised referencing the station operations work levels into the Australian Standards Framework. Their future work would be contracting private providers or TAFE to develop accredited workplace modules for all work streams in the industry. This scenario ended in an invitation to Sydney for a final update. It was my last free flight.

National Public Transport Training Board
7th Floor, 140 William St.
East Sydney, NSW 2011

Dennis Denman, Manager Training, Met Trains
Dear Dennis, re completion of Project 6.

On behalf of the Chairman & the Board, I would like to thank you ...

Yours sincerely
Sally-Ann Thomas, Executive Director.

Back to Metcard

The automatic ticketing and Metcard training had additionally enabled input into the equipment operating manuals. Provided by ERG (OneLink) we were able to modify the content into training manuals. The initial equipment set up in our facility had been fixed infrastructure, the Metcard (AT) vending machines, validating machines which would eventually be integrated into barriers enabling ticket only entry and exit from a station. The station booking office machine (ticket selling machine) keyed or authorised by a portable memory. The portable memory (PM) was basically an electronic identity card. Prior to the AT rollout, ERG began testing a portable validation machine that was proposed to be carried by CSEs and revenue protection officers. This latest piece of equipment led to another aspect of training which was undertaken at the CSE's city location at Flinders Street Station. The Met Trains station's workforce was prepared and ready.

Every member of the training group, Kevin, Gino, Derrick and Christina had contributed to different aspects of automatic ticketing. The rollout of Metcard occurred during the following months on the Alamein line as proposed. Bob Roberts and the ERG team had completed all the infrastructure at the stations between Camberwell and Alamein. The Ashburton station was the start point. I arrived at about 7:30 am to find Bob Roberts on hand and the equipment ticking over. CSEs were on hand in the role of hosts with a pocket full of ticket varieties to eliminate any embarrassment of ticket vending malfunctions. Line by line the program would be rolled out in the following years with our training customised to equipment on site.

The rollout was not without a degree of public reaction and some degree of worry with a significant failure rate on vending machines. Add in the smaller MVM1 vending machines on the non-premium stations were coin operated only. Rumours of customers staggering under the weight of coins were exaggerated but made for colourful images. There was a groundswell of perceived free rides as the city station barriers was locked up as the excuse of vending machines not working at a non-premium station became the norm. It was the start of something new and each day brought public acceptance as the rollout proceeded. Near year's end, my invite to The Point restaurant at Albert Park Lake read:

The Management and Staff of One Link would like to invite you to help celebrate the commissioning of Melbourne's Automated Ticketing System.

An easy invite to accept and a delight to circulate and be recognised as part of a broader team. A small recognition of another major project training outcome to add to my list. From the distance of Transport House, I shrugged as the role of the CSE was realigned much later from hosts to revenue protection. Another training need was now put forward by the revenue protection group on handling difficult customers and self-protection.

Did you hear the one about ...

The number of CSEs needed to apprehend a suspected ticket offender? Five. One on each leg, one on each arm and the fifth, asking for identification. As revenue was high on the business agenda, another training decision was appropriate but made off hand. It was a beat-up by the revenue protection officer classification and role that saw this group hypnotised by carrying a Freddie (a police type identifier) and believing at the time they were pseudo-cops. Notwithstanding that the transport act gave RIOs the scope to hold a suspect offender, albeit secured until the police arrived. The original concept of CSEs travelling in pairs has today been replaced by larger teams.

Top efforts rewarded

This was the heading in the PTC staff bulletin, but the performance of this small training group rarely made headlines. Met Trains has just completed a successful 12 months and Managing Director

Simon Lane made presentations at the year in review seminar. Among the achievements were:

- Completion of stage one of the Flinders Street Station upgrade
- Refurbishing of 25 premium station and non-premium stations
- Excellent revenue protection
- Improved services for special events
- NCSA 3-star safety ratings
- Significant increase in patronage.

As could be read by the content, the efficiencies within transport were well underway and other opportunities beckoned. This seminar was led by a PowerPoint presentation by Simon Lane for Met Trains, titled 'Building on Success'. It overviewed key performance levels and previewed the challenges for the year ahead and beyond including – privatisation.

The background on the business transformation program included a statement of purpose, goals in perspective (the strategic framework) and Met Trains, our guiding principles:

- Customer satisfaction
- The return to shareholders is vital to the organisation reputation
- Management decisions based on fact
- Problem-solving through teamwork
- The wellbeing of staff.

The drums were beating

Confirmed as the near future, privatisation and the way forward were clearly on target, with most non-Safeworking training seen as non-core business. That premise was never openly discussed or denied on the 15th floor. To others the message was clear and my peer training managers in both Met Tram and V/line Passenger negotiated exit packages. Both Greg and Frank had determined their futures and the benefit that a redundancy payout enabled. A great inter-mode working relationship concluded, almost overnight. Central to the general discussion was the individuals concern and 'how would it affect me'. Rumours of outsourcing of departments including payroll and other personal services including training were making the rounds. Spring Street were firm in their news statements that transport was crippling the State budget and privatisation would bring competition and improved services for the travelling community.

During the winter of '97 I had periods of disappearance as my mother's health condition continued to decline and she needed to be relocated between care facilities. Regrettably, in August 1997 she passed away. The support from the many of the personnel group was deeply appreciated. Christina had carried the position and was a readymade replacement. Her personality was open and engaging and she handled the hecklers with the same aplomb as she did her recently born daughter. After bereavement leave my return was short term before some staff moves changed our capacity. It was a busy period that would continue without some of its significant contributors. Kevin Giovannini had successfully won an operations role, and Gino some months later a position in Safeworking. They had determined their future outside of the training function. Mine was soon confirmed.

Privatisation

Privatisation became clear when the PTC formally split the suburban rail operations into Bayside Trains and Hillside Trains. V/line at the same time divided into V/Line Passenger and V/Line Freight. Behind closed doors the planning and resource allocation had been working overtime.

CHAPTER 16

HILLSIDE TRAINS – LAST HURRAH

My recollection is a little hazy but the outcome of a meeting with Peter Blackman was my transfer to Hillside Trains. Supposedly due to my experience in the train maintenance function and the rail signalling technology training centre. Conversely my time had run its course within this unit. Did I feel shafted with much of AT to be completed or of regrets in the shaping the training facility? It hardly crossed my mind. With the sale of the family home, I was independent of both Met Trains and Hillside. An instance of past rhetoric rekindled a smile.

> *All clerks, now includes managers and human resources, are bastards but not all bastards are …*

> Memo to S Tobias, J Sosa, C Semple, D Denman.
> Subject: interviews.
>
> As a consequence of appeals against the proposed appointments to the positions of Manager Education & Training within Bayside and Hillside trains, concurrent interviews had been scheduled for …. V Dalinkiewicz. A/ Manager Human Resources. April 1998

Another example of the PTC appeal process providing the most suitable applicant with natural justice.

The bells were tolling

I moved to another floor and found another group to assimilate into. The core of Hillside Trains personnel naturally mirrored Bayside with Barry James as the manager of personnel, or the more fashionable, human resources. This group had been carried over from workshops with the added responsibility of train operations. The suburban rail operations had effectively formed as a fully integrated business by geographical divide that included all maintenance depots and stabling. Hillside's share was the northern and western suburbs and sites. A new location and after many long years another window with sunlight. I had a comfortable window-side workstation shared with the OH&S officer and took a moment to reflect on the vagaries of a career. Here's cheers to that benevolent comedian who brought me back to a start point, albeit a small part of the workshops, nee Rolling Stock.

My responsibilities included the signals and communications staff and training centre located at Newport. They had been part of the parcel of infrastructure and personnel included with Hillside. Derrick DeSilva had additionally been part of the training divide. Derrick was possibly another on the wrong side of the age profile but had been a dedicated instructor and another of hidden talents, with a reputed office cleaning business and fresh egg supplier. Another invisible rail success story. I suggested rather than the isolation of Transport House he might be more comfortable with the trainers at Newport. As he lived in Werribee, a win all round. Much had happened in the decades of my departure from Champion Road.

Other events

In an article titled 'Workshops – where now?' Ann De Paul reports on the implementation of the strategy:

> *In 1986 the workshops business plan set out forecasts and objectives for the following five years. Group manager of engineering Dennis Smith said that Newport workshops would be rationalised and concentrated on the eastern half of the site. Staff reductions will save a total of $19.7 million annually with numbers falling from 2190 to 1473.*

The west block was surplus to operations and in much later years a number of roads would become the home of Steam Rail.

The Signals & Communication training centre at Newport was located within a small quadrant of the old workshops precinct and could be accessed by road from Shea Street, Newport. The six instructors' main priority was all aspects of rail signalling technology course, track environment safety and high voltage operator instruction. Ron Page undertook the high voltage (HV) training and was being utilised with contractor appreciation programs for the JDP. Noel Arnott, Mario Rodriquez and John Towler specialised in all signal's courses and aspects of equipment testing. Graeme Galletly undertook both contractor (fee for service) and industry rail protection courses. Ron Hessey, as the centre administration clerk, was our booking agent and purchasing guru. As a self-managed group, they needed a manager like an extra foot, but here I was.

The centre included a large area of dedicated track and track signalling infrastructure that enabled the ready transfer of theory to practice. On site an irreplaceable collection of essential equipment for rail control operations across all networks. I had some thoughts on their operations, resource and business cycles. Not quite an interloper but within a short time I had a second desk, had instigated an audit and shared some thoughts. On Level 12, in the privacy of backrooms, a detailed staff employee profile was surely being promulgated. Notwithstanding my role continued with maintaining the continuity of training services and the wider integrated business.

Roger Mendes, as the CEO, became the chief architect, supported by his senior managers. With the progress of JDP, the construction and commissioning of the McCauley maintenances depot and the Burnley light service and stabling sidings were being finalised. Add in Epping Maintenance Depot and I had a wide array of circulation options. And I did.

There but not there

I was never going to fit in with the James regime as it was soon apparent that we saw the world very differently and he already had his core of sycophants. After a 'his team' meeting where we clashed on an item, I was asked to return for a one on one. We agreed to disagree after I constructed a recent urgent report, required at two days' notice that his secretary had told me arrived 10 days previously on his desk. I understood he had more pressing matters, but alas he was better known in the industry for managing his son's AFL contracts than time management.

The needs of privatisation were many but my interests were elsewhere. There were tasks such as reviewing the training needs of the train maintainer and skilled, non-skilled roles for the sequence of service exams and heavy maintenance practices introduced by Dennis Smith to the Suburban Train Maintenance Review under Graeme Long. Déjà vu. Concurrent with this review was to recommend suitable supervisory training and options for a private provider or TAFE that could undertake on-site training.

The train ride to the depot was an easy distraction to talk to the Epping supervisors, confirming their responsibilities and learning the operation procedures. New sidings had been progressively built at Macaulay, Mordialloc, Carrum, Newport workshops and Burnley as the Jolimont yard rationalisation reached its final stage. Nearing completion, Westall was built as a major service depot and stabling site. The Hillside OH&S adviser was an energetic and conscientious practitioner and up to date with the latest OH&S acts and regulations. Westall saw him busy, with various commissioning and acceptance systems.

These locations all became part of my visits. As the new depots and their equipment were either commissioned and safety systems approved, the rail safety training needs at the new maintenance depots was an easy progression. With approval of the Superintendent of Safeworking, real time simulation for contractors in detonator use for rail protection was now conducted on site and on operating tracks between Williamstown and North

Williamstown. This same program was provided at the Westall depot for nominated staff and contractors.

The year was flashing by with the diploma taking a large proportion of my social time. To deny that some hours of study and submissions were completed during paid time would be a fib. Yet in the main, my study and write up periods included many weekends either at the University library or at Transport House. As with my period in Met Trains, many Sundays had been utilised in combining study and work schedules. Once more I used the Hillside resources of computing and printing over the period of my teaching diploma. These years later the building security was now best practice, but as a manager, my key system gave me access and always a passing chat with the security team.

Changing floors created a widening space from my past role and Christina my only contact as we discussed elements of mutual interest. The automatic ticketing program had now moved into the Northern and Western suburbs. She effectively became the remaining link of our successful teamwork of past years. Peter Blackman had assumed the Bayside CEO role as reputedly Simon Lane had moved to NSW Rail as that state planned the transport needs for the 2000 Olympics. With Bayside training facilities limited or replaced, I offered training rooms and facilities at the Newport Centre. With the welcome mat out, a series of CSE courses commenced.

Others were arranging equal opportunity information sessions (training) as part of the business unit meeting its compliance requirements (June 1999). How ironic, that in the mayhem of privatisation preparedness this program was to enable an understanding of your rights and the rights of others.

Equal Opportunity Act 1995 (Vic)

Equal opportunity included examples of harassment and discrimination, prohibited on the grounds of sex, pregnancy, race, marital status, disability, etc. It including two case studies:

- Jill's story: claimed she had been less favourably treated than others, during and after her period of maternity leave. Discrimination on the grounds of pregnancy.
- Bill's story: claimed he had been excluded from seeking job promotion because of his age and not capabilities. Discrimination on the grounds of age.

Deja vu. EO is not for you Denman, the position is redundant.

As the new business units formed there was a frenzy of activities to replicate a milliard of documents that required more than just a name and logo change. Selected programs for updating included the NSCA 3-star safety program, rail safety accreditation and the quality control system for documents. I was to head and tail (my) Met Trains Training and Education Policy and Guidelines Policy to a Hillside Trains quality documentation. Document: HET001.

Barry J found time to meet with the Newport Centre staff so I accompanied him and made the introductions. Faces were now linked to names and he left satisfied in their role. His office was bulging under due diligence documentation. My next distraction (and ego driven) was an application to the State Training Board of Victoria for the transfer to Hillside Trains as an accredited training organisation was approved with reservation. Off-site training, or away from Newport at times, upset the comfort of an instructor or two, echoing previous times and personnel. Unperturbed, together with Noel Arnott we co-wrote a Signals and Communication

Assessor program including a participant workbook. It was a rewarding experience to provide some structure to his high level of technical expertise. This assessor module was adapted from the workplace assessor program (Hawker de Havilland) of which we had approval. Add in a quarterly course directory designed by John Tolman and we increased our visibility. Published with proposed dates, it replaced the call around to prospective clients. Some wins, some not so.

Last throw at the stumps

Confirmation that I didn't fit in to the new regime – a vacancy for the position of Manager Safety Standards, Train Operation, Hillside Trains concluded with the following response from the Manager Train Operations.

> *Dear Dennis, screening against the specifications and qualifications for this particular position has led to the conclusion that your present qualifications and experience do not adequately match the position. Unfortunately, on this occasion the panel has decided against including you for further interview for the position.*
>
> *Yours sincerely, Manager Train Operations. September 1998.*

Let's try to be objective. I held a Graduate Diploma in Risk Management for Occupational Health & Safety, and had been involved with rail operation outcomes and Safeworking systems for a 10-year period including in joint ARU/management working parties. Admittedly I held no Safeworking briefs, but the role was obviously not as a signalman or a block and signal inspector.

Once more the theme, *all clerks are bastards, but not all bastards are clerks* shouted, enough is enough. Once more a segment from an earlier priority projects memorandum might have been perused. It was certainly within my personnel file. For the record without recrimination:

> He (D Denman) is also responsible for the oversight and coordination of the development of the Safeworking instructions and subsequent oversight of revisions necessitated by industrial and operation impacts.

Surely another inditement of a closed shops in operations continued, but other issues including the Hillside Trains – Privatisation Bulletin of May 1999 were of greater interest.

This particular bulletin was an invitation to all staff to attend our next round of privatisation/superannuation briefing sessions.

> *I will address you for about half an hour on two matters...Hillside's business issues and performance to date, followed by the second round of superannuation and financial information sessions.*
>
> Roger Mendes, Chief Executive Officer.

Due diligence

The process undertaken by all reputable organisations, and CGEA and MTC were undoubtably knee-deep in documents. In this regard, my contribution was a detailed resume of the value component of the training centre within Hillside. The human and physical resources at the signals and communication training centre at Newport were assessed as paramount to any purchasing entity.

To compliment this position, a meeting with a senior manager heading the government transport privatisation process confirmed their views on maintaining this core group within the MTC. A win for the Newport team and they were anointed 'work as usual'. The formality of that decision was in the hands of others.

Meanwhile, CGEA were also proactively selling its status as a leading international private operator of public transport services. The charm offensive and face of the company was led by Dale Larkin CGEA, Geoff Davis CGEA and Alan Cavanagh ALSTOM. They confirmed Melbourne Transport Enterprises as a subsidiary of CGEA that will operate the franchise of Hillside Trains and that MTE will contract with Alstom Australia for the rolling stock supply and for infrastructure and fleet maintenance.

My position, (Manager Training & Education) was tagged as surplus to requirements or redundant and I would be best suited to combine early retirement and the redundancy package. My age profile would now seem to be beneficial to both parties. All the numbers and best advice presented to me made the financial windfall the most beneficial option. After exhaustive sessions with the employee representative Michael Guiney, the projection was GO. I know that many (including myself) thanked Michael for his knowledge of the superannuation and his quiet assistance. I had signed the separation package nomination form which confirmed my position as surplus. It further detailed:

> *You will likely be operationally required until 28 August 1999. During this time, you may take advantage of the services provided by the Career Change Centre of the PTC.*

Those in the surplus bag had adequate time and assistance in detailing a proforma resume and an introduction to modern recruitment techniques. I was to spend the majority of the remaining period at Newport. A lunch on the lawn section of the Strand at Williamstown or a nearby pub was a latent pleasure. The drive across the Westgate Bridge, long established as the gateway to the west, became a cathartic time as the past and present momentarily fused as my time concluded. Still, I had little spare time as I was completing the last two modules of my Education & Training Diploma. By year's end, I graduated.

Other events

The Kennett Government's privatisation program was a step away from conclusion. The information flow was a steady stream from the Office of Premier & Minister for Public Transport.

> *NEWS RELEASE 13 July: New public transport investment to top $1.6 Billion. Premier, Mr Kennett, announced today that the private sector investment in Victoria's public transport system will top $1.6 billion with the awarding of the Hillside Train franchise to Melbourne Transport Enterprises.*

Last hurrah

My reflection in the mirror confirmed my age profile and what a great ride it had been. As the 'Peter Principle' so rightly predicted my time had come. I had been involved in a period of great change in the rail industry of Victoria. Better still, I worked as part of successive teams that altered the face of rail operations on distant freight lines and the suburban system that had been linked by the underground below Melbourne's CBD.

I had managed and formed working relationships with many different people and groups over many years to my personal gain and hopefully others to a small degree. To those who would disagree, to whit, some training managers are bastards, but not all bastards are ... I can but agree.

Training as an essential cog of any enterprise had moved with the times and is today mostly nationally accredited. Self-development was a normal part of my working life but regrettably not taken up by many who hid behind the operations veil. Many of my managers were 'rail trained' administrators, accountants, engineers or operations, but lacked management accreditation. I left an industry moving towards privatisation and many years later is unrecognisable from the benevolent bureaucracy, The Victorian Railways. My greatest pleasure over my time was at the electrical training centre with that core of individuals and the youth of an industry, but alas, the manual training centres are long gone. But other involvements and participation are irreplaceable such as my time in major transport reforms and multiple projects. Sometimes it's enough to be a bit player, a contributor on the chessboard, albeit there will only be one king.

On 28 August, a week before my 55th birthday, I quietly left Transport House. My home journey to Hawthorn was once more by tram.

On Saturday 18 September 1999, the Kennett government was defeated by Steve Bracks in the Victorian state election, although it would take another four weeks, as three independents negotiated as a block to reject another term of Kennett and enable Bracks to form the 54th parliament of Victoria. The franchises for the divided metropolitan rail services were not all smooth running with National Express (Bayside trains) handing in its franchise in December 2002. In 2003 the State Government began negotiations to operate the trains as a single entity, awarding the contract to Connex Melbourne. Today, it is Metro Trains Melbourne.

Some changes may be expected, author, 2022

POSTSCRIPT

Another Denman had preceded me in this industry. Joseph Denman had joined the Victorian Railways as a lad trainee from Ballarat in 1921. His journey was not quite as smooth as mine although he may have thought otherwise. My father's early childhood years had seen him exposed to personal family tragedy that was never shared. Much was only to be revealed by a long period of research long after his death. Born in Boulder, Western Australia his mother and his siblings had relocated to Ballarat on the death of his father in a mining accident. He had commenced his working life separated from his family like many young men and apprentices at Newport workshops.

Twelve months later, his classification as a trainee train examiner and his location and roles were on the move. On his history sheet, his work locations resembled a travel itinerary as he was sent to the far reaches of the state. He was to spend the better part of a decade on the relief rosters, spending time at all of the locations listed: Ballarat workshops, East Melbourne car shop, Cressy, North Melbourne car & wagon shop, Ararat, C&W shop, Bairnsdale, Warragul, Moe, Traralgon, North Melbourne car & wagon shop, Stawell car & wagon shop, Ballarat East, Shepparton, Benalla, Nyora, Korumburra, Ballarat loco and Ballarat Station yard.

The particulars of his 'running fowl' of management is today reflective of youth and a bureaucratic system. Commendatory & Punishment entries:

Fined 5 shillings for travelling without a ticket, Newport to Melbourne.

Cautioned for misconduct at Newport w/shops, failed to lift his token before starting work.

Fined 2/6 at Ballarat workshops at 4.52 pm, was washing his hands.

Many other entries should remain undisclosed for their banality and reflection of the times. (Source FOI)

The Victorian Railway Institute family was an integral part of his life where he used its many facilities and made friends across the state. He was to be gutted again with the death of his first wife within six years of his marriage. His working life revolved around shift work and a system of Yes sir to No sir. The steam train and open wagon freight had been the predominate features of his work roles before the introduction of diesel locomotives and bulk trains began a new era. If asked to nominate his most disliked posting ... without a moment's hesitation: 'Cressy, the arse hole of the world.'

Regrettably, with his early death, we were never to share more stories of a wheel tapper and his days at many branch lines and country depots before their curtain call.

JOSEPH DENMAN: Commenced Victorian Railways 4/10/1921. Dec. 27/4/1966.

www.ingramcontent.com/pod-product-compliance
Lightning Source LLC
Chambersburg PA
CBHW030108100526
44591CB00009B/322